WITHDRAWN

Buddhism,
the
First Millennium

Buddhism,
the
First Millennium

Daisaku Ikeda

translated by Burton Watson

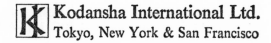 Kodansha International Ltd.
Tokyo, New York & San Francisco

Distributed in the United States by Kodansha International/USA, Ltd. through Harper & Row, Publishers, Inc., 10 East 53rd Street, New York, New York 10022. In South America by Harper & Row, International Department. In Canada by Fitzhenry & Whiteside Limited, 150 Lesmill Road, Don Mills, Ontario. In Mexico & Central America by Harla S.A. de C.V., Apartado 30–546, Mexico 4, D.F. In the United Kingdom by Phaidon Press Limited, Littlegate House, St. Ebbe's Street, Oxford OX1 1SQ. In Europe by Boxerbooks Inc., Limmatstrasse 111, 8031 Zurich. In Australia & New Zealand by Book Wise (Australia) Pty. Ltd., 104–8 Sussex Street, Sydney 2000. In the Far East by Toppan Company (S) Pte. Ltd., Box 22 Jurong Town Post Office, Jurong, Singapore 22.

Published by Kodansha International Ltd., 2–12–21 Otowa, Bunkyo-ku, Tokyo 112 and Kodansha International/USA, Ltd., 10 East 53rd Street, New York, New York 10022 and 44 Montgomery Street, San Francisco, California 94104. Copyright © 1977 by Daisaku Ikeda.
All rights reserved. Printed in Japan.

LCC 77–84915
ISBN 0–87011–321–6
JBC 1015–786186–2361

First edition, 1977

Contents

CONTENTS

Preface

In February, 1961, I stood on the banks of the Ganges, that mighty river that begins as a tiny trickle of clear water among the Himalayas, the "roof of the world," and races down from their towering peaks, traversing the foothills, to water the vast plain of the Hindustan. Near the city of Patna, where I was standing, it gathers into itself a number of large and small tributary streams. Close to this spot in ancient times stood Pataliputra, the "City of Flowers," capital of the Maurya dynasty, the first kingdom to extend its rule over almost all of the Indian continent.

The sacred Ganges flows on today, just as it did so long ago when Shakyamuni, having finished preaching the most important series of sermons on the Dharma or Buddhist Truth to his disciples at Vulture Peak, crossed over it from the village of Patali, heading northward on foot in the direction of his old home of Kapilavastu. He was nearing the time of his death, a fact which he no doubt realized. I wonder what he thought about as he stood alone by the Ganges. Standing and looking out over the vast surging waters, I tried to imagine what might have been in the heart of the Buddha.

For how many countless centuries has the river continued day after day to flow in this fashion? As long as the waters of life well up upon the earth, it will go on flowing. The profound and time-less wisdom of Shakyamuni, born in Lumbini in the foothills of the Himalayas, like the Ganges continued for over a thousand years to flow through the land of the Indian people. And from there it spread south to Sri Lanka, southeast to the regions of Burma, Thailand, and Cambodia, northward through Central Asia and along the Silk

Road into China, and by way of the Korean peninsula into Japan. Moreover, in the time of King Ashoka in the third century B.C., Buddhist monks journeyed as envoys to the various Greek states of the Macedonian empire, so that from early times it was already known to the West as well.

Shakyamuni, that extraordinary man of ancient times, died long ago, but he left behind a body of teachings such as the world had never known. And these teachings, born of the passionate desire to save mankind that dominated his entire life, were handed down from one disciple to another, from one follower to ten thousand, until they became a vast current of faith transcending national boundaries.

Since my visit to India, the land where Buddhism was born, I have thought increasingly of the early history of the faith and have felt a desire to try to put down in writing some of my ideas concerning the man Shakyamuni, the founder of the faith. I was able to realize a part of my desire a few years ago, writing a book entitled *Watakushi no Shakusonkan* or "My View of the Buddha," which has been translated into English under the title *The Living Buddha*.

Needless to say, the Buddhist religion is not the possession of Shakyamuni alone. Just as the life force of the Buddha has existed, and will continue to exist, for all time, so the Buddhist religion is a faith that aims at the salvation of all human beings everywhere. After Shakyamuni's death, his disciples gathered together to put into formal shape the teachings he had left behind, and thus in time was formed that huge mass of scriptures and commentaries that make up the Buddhist canon. Among them are the scriptures of Mahayana Buddhism, in particular the Lotus Sutra, which were formed at the hands of lay believers who strove to realize the bodhisattva ideal by working to diffuse Buddhism more widely throughout society. Each of these later disciples and followers of the religion drew upon the life force of the eternal Buddha as it existed within his own being and pressed forward to the best of his ability toward the realm of enlightenment, the realm of the Buddha.

In my earlier volume I surveyed the life of Shakyamuni. In the present one I would like to continue to trace the history of Buddhism, examining its early development in India and endeavoring to define the basic principles and ideals of the religion. As in the case of the earlier volume, I have drawn with gratitude upon numerous excellent studies published by Buddhologists and Indologists, and I wish here to express my gratitude to them for their endeavors in the past and, as a Buddhist, to pray for the continued success of their researches in the future.

I would like in closing to express my thanks to Burton Watson, adjunct professor of Columbia University, for the pains he has taken in preparing the translation, and to the staff of Kodansha International Ltd. for their labor and patience in producing the book.

Translator's Note

The present volume is a translation of a work in Japanese entitled *Watakushi no Bukkyōkan* or "My View of Buddhism" (Tokyo: Daisan bummeisha, 1974). The original work was cast in the form of a discussion between Mr. Ikeda and two of his associates, but with his permission I have, for purposes of smoother reading, recast it in straight narrative form, taking care of course to preserve all the factual and speculative material of the original.

Sanskrit and Pali personal names, place names, and technical terms have been introduced in the text in the romanized form that seems most suitable for ordinary English readers, without the elaborate diacritical marks demanded by strict Indology. Nearly all such names and terms have, however, been listed in the glossary with full diacritical marks, indications as to which terms are Sanskrit and which Pali, and, in the case of the more important, their Japanese pronunciations or equivalents. Doctrinal terms in both English and Japanese are also explained in the glossary. Names of modern (post-1868) Japanese individuals are given in the text in Western fashion, personal name preceding family name.

As indicated by Mr. Ikeda in his preface to the English edition, the present work is a sequel to his earlier volume, *The Living Buddha: An Interpretive Biography* (New York & Tokyo: Weatherhill, 1976), which deals with Shakyamuni, the founder of Buddhism. Treating as it does the life of a single individual, *The Living Buddha* is unified in subject and has a clear beginning, middle, and end. Moreover, Shakyamuni's life, though marked at times by hardship and sadness, was on the whole a relatively untroubled one that ended on a triumphant note of accomplishment and optimism, and this sunniness is reflected in Mr. Ikeda's treatment.

The present volume concerns itself with the story of Buddhism in the dark days after the death of Shakyamuni. It is perforce more diverse in content, covers a vastly greater span of time, and is in some ways more somber in tone, for, as so often happens in the history of religion, once the founder of the new faith had passed from the scene, doubt and dissension arose among his followers. Controversy developed concerning the correct interpretation of the doctrine, the correct practices and goals for the monks and laity, and the Buddhist order in time was torn by schism. Mr. Ikeda, himself the leader of Soka Gakkai, a vast and rapidly growing religious lay organization affiliated with the Nichiren Shoshu sect of Buddhism, describes these problems that beset early Buddhism, piecing out the scant historical facts with insight and conjecture. He succeeds in casting new light upon a period in the history of Buddhism that, because of the paucity of reliable data, is shrouded in uncertainty, bringing the account of its development down to the point where it had begun to spread beyond the borders of India and to grow into a major world religion.

1

The Formation
of the Buddhist Canon

The First Council

In an earlier volume I have discussed the events of Shakyamuni's
life. I propose now to examine the development of Buddhism in the
period that followed. Immediately after Shakyamuni's death, we
are told by the scriptures, his followers gathered together with the
purpose of putting his teachings and sermons into definitive order.
It is impossible to determine the exact date of his death, though it
probably took place around the fifth or sixth century B.C. Since we
are dealing with events that transpired well over two thousand years
ago, we cannot hope to learn of them in detail. Our only recourse
is to examine the fragmentary bits of information recorded in the
Buddhist scriptures, piece them out with conjecture, and in this
manner attempt to reconstruct the way in which the Buddhist canon
came into being.

The First Council, as this gathering of the disciples is called, is said
to have taken place in the year of Shakyamuni's death, at a place
called Saptaparna-guha or The Cave of the Seven Leaves in a
mountainside near Rajagaha, the capital of the state of Magadha.
It was attended by some five hundred monks and centered about
Mahakashyapa, Ananda, Upali, and the others among Shakyamuni's Ten Major Disciples who were still alive at the time. We
are told that Ajatashatru, the king of Magadha, also lent his assis-
tance to the council. The site remains in existence today, and photographs of it show a gently sloping hill with a cave in the side, ap-
proached by a flight of some ten stone steps. One can make out a
broad open area within, where the members of the council gathered
in order to be protected from the rain.

Some Western scholars of Buddhism question whether the First Council ever in fact took place. However, the scriptures of both Theravada and Mahayana Buddhism mention "the rules formulated at the gathering of the five hundred," or "the five hundred who compiled the precepts," indicating that such a gathering occurred. We may, of course, deny the validity of the scriptures themselves, in which case, since they are our only source, we are reduced to silence. Most Buddhist scholars, however, at least in Japan, regard the First Council as a historical fact.

With the death of such an extraordinary leader, it is only natural to suppose that Shakyamuni's disciples should want to gather together immediately and put into order their recollections of his teachings so that the Dharma or Law, the truths of the Buddhist religion, could be handed down to later generations without error.

The scriptures record an interesting episode concerning the particular circumstances that impelled Mahakashyapa to call the members of the Order together in council. According to this account, Mahakashyapa, accompanied by a large group of monks, was on his way from Pava to Kushinagara at the time when Shakyamuni, who had gone ahead of him to Kushinagara, passed away. Along the road Mahakashyapa and his group met a Brahman, who was holding in his hand a *mandara* flower. Mahakashyapa asked him if he had any news of Shakyamuni, whereupon the man replied that Shakyamuni was no longer of this world. Hearing this, some of the monks began to weep and wail aloud, while others grieved in silence. To everyone's astonishment, however, one old monk burst into the following embittered harangue. "Friends, cease your sorrow, cease your grieving!" he cried. "Now we are free at last from that Great Monk. 'This you may do,' he would say to us, or 'This is not proper for you,' making life miserable for us and oppressing us. But now we may do whatever we like and need never do anything that goes against our wishes!"

Mahakashyapa, who was known in the Order as "foremost in ascetic practices," naturally listened to these rantings with grave displeasure. As soon as the funeral of Shakyamuni had taken place and his remains had been taken care of, he addressed the other monks in these words: "Friends, we must make certain that the teachings and ordinances are put into proper form, rendering it impossible for false doctrines to flourish while true ones decline, for false ordinances to be set up while true ones are discarded, for

14

expounders of false teachings to grow strong while expounders of the truth grow weak, for expounders of false ordinances to seize power while expounders of true ones lose it."

Mahakashyapa, we are told, selected five hundred monks to undertake the task of putting Shakyamuni's sermons and teachings in order and shaping them into the canon of the Buddhist religion.

The account, when we consider it, seems plausible enough. And the anecdote serves to point up one important motive that lay behind the compilation of the canon. I am referring, of course, to the notoriously unpredictable nature of the human heart. Among Shakyamuni's followers were those who ordinarily evinced the greatest respect for him and were diligent and strict in their practice of the Dharma or Law. And yet in certain cases they retained in their hearts a fundamental egoism and narrowness of vision. Faced with the fact of Shakyamuni's death, the true nature of their hearts was suddenly and almost unconsciously revealed to view. That, I believe, is what the story of the old monk and his shocking outburst is intended to convey.

To his disciples, Shakyamuni was a teacher of the way of life, one who bestowed on them the deep compassion and love of a father, while at the same time he was the leader of their religious organization. The large majority of his disciples regarded him with awe and respect, but there must have been others who could not live up to the severe discipline demanded of them, the ordinances that made their lives so different from those of ordinary laymen, and who were still prey to the temptations and delusions of the mundane world. It was only natural for such persons to feel, however mistakenly, that they had been liberated from an oppressive spiritual burden. The rantings of the old monk served as a warning to Mahakashyapa that a certain atmosphere of liberation and even laxness was likely to invade the Order.

The death of its foremost leader meant that the Order faced a time of grave peril, for, in the Indian society of the period, still overwhelmingly dominated by the various sects of Brahmanism, Buddhism was as yet a very new religion and one with a relatively small following. The death of the founder naturally deprived the organization of its prime source of leadership and inspiration and plunged many of the disciples into a mood of deepest despair. They undoubtedly felt a sudden emptiness in their hearts, a sense of fathomless bewilderment and loss.

Shakyamuni's passing probably occasioned varied reactions among persons and groups outside the Buddhist Order as well. Those who looked upon the new religion with ill will in all likelihood predicted that it would signal gradual disintegration, for no matter how outstanding a personality the founder of a new religious order may be, if he can find no suitable successor to carry on his work, the order is likely to be troubled by internal dissension and related problems and to fall into a decline. The various Brahmanical sects in particular, we may surmise, hoped and believed that this was what would occur.

This is not surprising, since it appears to have been the general belief that there was no one in the Buddhist Order at the time who was of truly exceptional stature. The scriptures record the following exchange which took place when the disciple Ananda chanced to meet an old friend who was a Brahman. "Ananda," the Brahman inquired, "now that the Buddha has passed away, is there anyone of equal stature to carry on in his place?"

Ananda replied, "Friend, how could there possibly be anyone of equal greatness? The Buddha through his own efforts attained an understanding of the Truth and set about putting it into practice. All that we, his disciples, can do is to follow the teachings that he handed down and the example that he set for us."

In other words, "Rely on the Law, not on the person," as the Buddhist phrase has it. Just as the earlier anecdote concerning Mahakashyapa indicated that a definitive Buddhist canon was necessary for the solidarity and maintenance of the religious order, so this one concerning Ananda illustrates the necessity for such a canon as an authoritative foundation in matters of faith.

We are told in the Nirvana Sutra that Shakyamuni just before his death addressed the disciples gathered about him in the following words: "Although I may die, you must not for that reason think that you are left without a leader. The teachings and precepts I have expounded to you shall be your leader. Therefore if any of you have any doubts, now is the time to question me about them. You must not lay yourself open to regret later on, when you may say, 'Why didn't we ask him while he was still alive!'" Shortly after, he said, "Decay is inherent in all composite things. Work out your own salvation with diligence." These famous words were his final pronouncement as he passed into nirvana.

It is from this passage that the precept "Rely on the Law, not on the person" derives. Shakyamuni no doubt intended his words to be a warning against the self-appointed teachers who would come forward after his death and attempt to confound the doctrine with their own private interpretations and theories. There are some Buddhist scholars who believe that work had already begun upon the compilation of a definitive canon during Shakyamuni's lifetime, though the more common view is that he merely charged his disciples to keep a careful record in their minds of his words and actions. This is probably why, during his later years, he kept Ananda, who was famed for remarkable powers of memory, constantly by his side as his personal attendant. Nearly all the sutras begin in their Chinese versions with a phrase that means "Thus have I heard." In nearly all cases the "I," we are told, represents Ananda, who recited from memory the words that he had heard the Buddha preach.

Jainism, another new religion that arose in India at about the same time as Buddhism or slightly earlier, split into two divisions after the death of its founder because, it is said, there was no definitive canon to appeal to in cases of doctrinal dispute. Some scholars suggest that it was this example which led Shakyamuni to charge Shariputra, another of his principal disciples, with the task of codifying his teachings.

There can be no doubt that Shakyamuni, particularly in his late years, gave intense thought to the question of how best to "insure the continued existence of the Dharma," as the traditional phrase expresses it. Any religious leader of outstanding ability and foresight can be expected to give serious and constant consideration to the future of the organization after his death. The proof that Shakyamuni did so is to be found in the fact that, immediately after his departure from the world, his followers came together in conclave and put his teachings in order. This act, together with the immense amount of effort expended by members of the Buddhist faith over the following thousand years or more in preserving and enlarging the body of sacred scriptures, are surely reflections of the intense concern that Shakyamuni evinced during his lifetime for the "continued existence of the Dharma."

The Recitation of the Words of the Buddha

As has already been mentioned, the scriptures contain various notices concerning the First Council, "the assembly of five hundred monks and nuns," as one describes it. From these we learn that Mahakashyapa, eldest of the surviving major disciples, acted as chairman of the conference, while the disciples Ananda and Upali were chosen to recite the words of the Buddha as they had memorized them. Ananda, having been for a long period of time the personal attendant of Shakyamuni and constantly at his side, was in a position to remember just what teachings the Buddha had expounded, where, and to whom, while Upali, who was noted among the Ten Major Disciples as "foremost in *vinaya* or discipline," possessed the most thorough knowledge of the rules of discipline the Buddha had laid down for the Order. Thus Ananda recited before the assembly the words pertaining to the Dharma, which came to be referred to as sutras, while Upali dictated the rules and regulations that are known collectively as the *vinaya*.

We may be certain, however, that it was not simply their powers of memory and recall that qualified Ananda and Upali for the task assigned them. Rather it was because they were in a sense living embodiments of the Buddha's teachings. Anyone who is sincerely desirous of learning the Truth and who works with his whole being to absorb and retain every word and phrase that is taught to him will find it impossible ever after to divorce himself from such teachings, even if he should wish to do so. Thus although his teacher may die, he can still hear the voice of his teacher resounding within his own body. The term *shōmon*, meaning those who have "heard the voice," is used to describe those disciples who were able to listen to Shakyamuni's preaching. Such men, when they could no longer listen to the actual voice of Shakyamuni, no doubt kept continually in remembrance his teachings as they were engraved upon the inner being of each individual and continued to pursue the religious life in the light of such teachings.

Needless to say, there were in those days no mechanical means of recording nor any methods of taking shorthand. It is even doubtful that scripts existed for the writing of Indian languages.[1] Shakya-

1. The oldest examples of Indian writing (excepting the ancient Harappa inscriptions) date from the third century B.C. In the preceding centuries, litera-

muni's disciples, if they were to retain his teachings, had no recourse but to make those teachings an integral part of their own being.

It is important to note that these teachings are not in any sense a system of intellectual knowledge or a body of facts. Rather they are an expression of wisdom addressed to such questions as how man ought to live or what is the cause of human suffering. As the disciples received the teachings of the Buddha, they proceeded to put them into practice in their own lives and in this way one by one verified the truth and validity of Shakyamuni's words.

The teachings of Buddhism, we must remember, are to be mastered subjectively, through actual practice. One can never understand them by sitting at a desk and reading a book. Only through the exchange that takes place between one person and another, one life force and another life force, can their truths be grasped. This point should also be kept in mind when approaching the Buddhist scriptures, which represent the embodiment of the teachings and wisdom.

We may suppose that Upali in his daily attitudes and activities exemplified the rules of conduct and discipline laid down for the Buddhist Order. It was not that he went about recalling to mind one by one the ordinances that Shakyamuni had formulated, but rather that all of his actions had unconsciously come to be a living expression of the discipline or *vinaya* and of the spirit that underlay it. Had he not mastered it so thoroughly, it is unlikely that he would have been singled out among all the disciples for the epithet "foremost in *vinaya*."

Something similar can probably be said of Ananda. So thoroughly had he absorbed the preachings of the Buddha that in a sense they flowed forth from every part of his body. If he had not had this mastery of them, he would not have been able to recite from memory such a vast number of sermons, a feat that is indeed one of the wonders of the history of Buddhism. As we shall see later, the Tripitaka or Buddhist canon consists of three parts: the sutras or preachings of the Buddha, the *vinayas* or rules of discipline, and the *shastras* or commentaries. Of these, the sutras, which were recited by Ananda, run to over six thousand volumes.

ture was handed down orally, as seems to have been the case with the early Buddhists, and the men of the time were no doubt capable of feats of memory that would seem incredible to us today. Tr.

19

The scriptures describe the circumstances under which the canon was compiled in the following manner. We are told that Mahaka-shyapa addressed the two disciples who were to be the reciters, saying: "Monks, listen to my words. I believe the time has come for us to question the elder monk Ananda concerning the doctrines of the faith."

To this Ananda replied, "Monks, listen to my words. I believe the time has come for me to reply to the questions of the elder monk Mahakashyapa concerning the doctrines of the faith."

Mahakashyapa then asked, "My friend Ananda, where did the Buddha preach his first sermon?"

Ananda once more replied, saying, "My friend Mahakashyapa, thus have I heard. The Buddha was once at the Deer Park in Banaras. . . ."

When Ananda then went on to describe how Shakyamuni delivered his famous first sermon at the Deer Park at present-day Sarnath near Benares, we are told that the older monks all began to weep and sank to the ground in grief. It must have been an awesome and moving scene. So deep was their sorrow over the death of Shakyamuni that, when Ananda recreated the words of the sermon, and the noble figure of Shakyamuni appeared once more in memory as he had been in life, they were overcome with emotion.

It is recorded that after Ananda had completed his recitation, the members of the gathering examined it to make certain that it contained no errors, and then all recited it together in unison, each monk in this way engraving the words upon his mind.

This group recitation is of particular importance, for it was in this way that each member of the council committed the words of the sermon to memory, enabling him to then hand them on to others. According to scholars, the various hymns and other rhymed portions of the sutras were worked out by the members of the council in order to make the words of the Buddha easier to memorize. Also, since paper did not exist at this time and it was impossible to write down the texts of the sermons, it was necessary that each recitation should be submitted to the careful scrutiny of the assembly. Only when a version that all could consent to had been reached would the joint recitation take place. Because of the way in which it was carried out, the work of the First Council is sometimes described as "the first group recitation," as well as "the first compilation" of the scriptures.

Here we must note that Buddhism stresses the necessity of reading or reciting the sutras with the three activities of "body, mouth, and mind." In other words, as stated earlier, the important thing is not to approach them like a body of intellectual knowledge, such as might be done in the West, but to discover how one can make the Buddha's teachings a part of one's self and put them into actual practice.

It is natural to suppose that in any group of persons listening to the teachings of the Buddha, such as the five hundred monks at the First Council, there are bound to be differences in the manner in which the different individuals apprehend these teachings. Some of the monks had perhaps heretofore interpreted certain of the teachings in an arbitrary manner so as to accord with their own predilections. Others, perhaps, because of their innate temperament, had completely mistaken the gist of all of Shakyamuni's words. The coming together of the five hundred, the examination of each point in the teachings with the utmost care, and the establishment of a definitive version of the Buddha's words which all the members of the assembly could give their assent to, and which in the future would be the common property of the religious order as a whole, are of enormous significance in the history of Buddhism.

Through this first codification of the teachings, it was hoped that a unity of doctrine and opinion might be established within the religious order at a time when death had deprived it of its founder and leader. On the basis of the extant sources it is possible to surmise that the aim was not necessarily to collect all the various teachings expounded by Shakyamuni during the course of his life, but to give precedence to those that seemed of greatest importance and usefulness in the immediate preservation and continuance of the religious order. (This is a point I shall have occasion to refer to again later when I come to discuss the formation of the Mahayana scriptures.)

I have earlier related an anecdote from the scriptures telling how Ananda was asked by a Brahman friend if there was someone worthy to succeed Shakyamuni, and how he replied in the negative. We find a very similar anecdote concerning Ananda and a high minister of the state of Magadha. "Ananda," asked the minister, "has someone been designated by the Buddha to be the leader of the monks in the period after his departure?"

"No, Your Lordship, there is no such person."

"Then is there someone whom the elder monks have agreed to recognize and support as an authority for the monks to rely upon in the period after the Buddha's departure?"

"No, Your Lordship, there is no such person."

"Then, Ananda, what will the monks rely upon, and how will they maintain concord within the Order?"

To this Ananda replied with firmness and confidence: "Your Lordship, we are by no means without anything to rely upon. Your Lordship, we have something to rely upon. The Law is what we rely upon!"

From this we may see that the canon compiled at the First Council served as a basis of absolute authority. The monks referred to the teachings of the Buddha thus preserved by the term *agama*, which means "sacred teachings," and cherished them as something to be relied upon without question.

These earliest sacred scriptures, referred to within the larger context of Buddhist writings as the *agonbu* or *agama* division, devote a great deal of attention to precepts and rules of discipline. Some scholars even go so far as to suggest that the *agama* were in fact compiled principally to serve as a book of rules for the Buddhist monasteries.

Why these early scriptures should be of this nature can be partly explained by the circumstances surrounding their compilation— the general feeling, as we have seen, that there was no person worthy to act as Shakyamuni's successor in leading the new religious organization and that therefore reliance was to be placed upon the teachings and precepts handed down by Shakyamuni. In addition, the scriptures may well reflect the temperament of the particular monks who assembled at the conclave, especially those of Mahakashyapa and the other elders who acted as leaders of the council.

Mahakashyapa, as noted in the description of him in my earlier volume, was singled out among the Ten Major Disciples as "foremost in *dhuta* or ascetic practice," an indication that, though surely not fanatical, he was very strict in his observance of the various austerities enjoined by Shakyamuni. But although he was capable of excelling the other disciples in his devotion to ascetic practice, he does not otherwise seem to have been a very colorful personality. Surely he never enjoyed the kind of infectious popularity that Shariputra and Maudgalyayana aroused among the members of the Order, and I have the feeling that he was probably somewhat deficient in an understanding of the deeper philosophical principles of Shakyamuni's teachings. As long as Shariputra and Maudgal-yayana remained alive, it appears to have been a common assumption that they would be Shakyamuni's successors, though, as it happened, both men preceded Shakyamuni in death. Mahaka-shyapa, however, was apparently never considered to be of the stature worthy to qualify as Shakyamuni's heir. Even his friend Ananda, as we have seen earlier, had to admit that there was in fact no one among the remaining disciples distinguished enough for that role.

This is not to deny that Mahakashyapa played a crucial and praiseworthy part in the convening and proceedings of the First Council. Yet the fact that a person such as he was chosen to head the council suggests that the standards for selecting the participants were questionable in nature.

For example, Purna, another major disciple, was not among those selected. He is said to have remarked that he intended to carry out the teachings of the Buddha in accordance with the way he himself had heard them expounded by Shakyamuni. The statement, although it does not directly challenge the authority of the First Council, suggests that he, and perhaps others like him, had reservations about the way in which Mahakashyapa and his fellow council members were codifying the teachings. It would also appear that there were a considerable number of Shakyamuni's followers who were unable to attend the First Council but who carried on their religious activities independently in various outlying regions. Later we will have occasion to discuss the Mahayana sutras that took shape in the following centuries. It is quite possible that they were put together by these smaller religious groups that did not choose to be limited by the canon as it was formulated by the majority of the Order at the First Council.

Reviewing the events of this period, one may see what a severe blow it was to the Order that both Shariputra and Maudgalyayana should have died before Shakyamuni. Shakyamuni himself was reported to have said, "Since Shariputra and Maudgalyayana died, this gathering seems empty to me!" Their loss no doubt inflicted upon him incalculable sorrow.

If these two remarkable men had taken part in the First Council, it is quite possible that the early Buddhist canon would have assumed a somewhat different form. While it is perhaps idle to speculate at this late date, we should recall that, in Shakyamuni's closing years, both men were permitted to preach the Dharma in his stead, so well versed were they in the theory as well as the practice of the new religion. They were in fact the two great pillars of the Order, and if they had survived to become the leaders after Shakyamuni's death, Buddhism might have developed in a quite different manner from that in which it did.

However that may be, the fact is that, in the historical growth of Buddhism in this early period, it was the canon fixed by the First Council that served as the core of the faith, being regarded with the utmost reverence and gravity. And, although the canon may have had its imperfections and deficiencies, the determination of the men who compiled it to "insure the continuance of the Dharma" was the factor that led in time to the birth of the whole great corpus of Buddhist teachings.

That we can read the sutras and discover in them the doctrines derived from the wisdom of the Buddha is due to the action and precedent set by the early disciples in gathering together immediately after Shakyamuni's death to put the canon into order. For this reason we cannot but look to them with feelings of deep gratitude. The intense concern which Mahakashyapa, Ananda, and the others showed over the preservation and continuance of the Dharma is what made it possible for Buddhism to survive and to be handed down over the twenty some centuries until today.

The Teachings of Great Religious Leaders

The great men of history generally leave behind them a record in some form or other of their actions and words. Some of them, particularly the politicians, take the precaution of compiling their own memoirs and biographies so as to show themselves to posterity in the best possible light. These last works, smacking as they do of self-justification, are seldom read for long, whatever attention they may attract when they appear. Yet four of the greatest men in all history, Shakyamuni, Socrates, Confucius, and Jesus of Nazareth, left no writings whatsoever from their own hand. In their case, the records of their words and deeds were compiled by their disciples, and these records have served as an unending source of inspiration for over two thousand years of human civilization.

In the case of Socrates and Jesus, because both in a sense met with tragic deaths, it is highly likely that their biographies have been considerably dramatized at the hands of their disciples. Thus, as scholars have long pointed out, the picture of Socrates facing death that is built up by Plato in the *Crito*, *Phaedo*, and the *Apology*, and the account of the crucifixion and resurrection of Jesus as it is recorded in the Gospels contain elements at variance with historical fact.

By comparison, the portrayal of Shakyamuni in the early Buddhist scriptures conveys a striking sense of realism and simple humanity. In the Mahayana scriptures, however, the account of the Buddha becomes highly elaborated and overlaid with literary embellishments. Western scholars may find such elaborations difficult to comprehend, and may well prefer the earlier accounts. I myself, however, and most other Eastern Buddhists, are overwhelmingly drawn to the Buddha of the Mahayana scriptures.

Buddhologists both in Asia and the West, reflecting the positivism and critical approach of modern Western scholarship, have in recent years devoted great effort to discovering the historical facts underlying the traditional accounts. Needless to say, I applaud such efforts and hope to see them carried forward with all possible diligence.

Still I would like to express a word of caution and reservation concerning the methodology employed by some of these modern researchers. In what they claim to be an objective search for historical fact, they seem intent upon employing the standards and viewpoints of modern man to lay bare the true personalities of the great men of history. If their methods do in fact succeed in constructing a clearer and more truthful portrait of the great man, one which can be more deeply appreciated and understood by those of us living today, then their efforts are all to the good. But too often the opposite seems to be true. The scholars appear deliberately to ignore aspects of greatness and to focus all attention upon failings, as though they were determined to drag the subject of their inquiry down to the level of the ordinary human being. I sense behind their endeavors a kind of arrogance toward the past that is characteristic of modern man.

The traditional accounts of Shakyamuni, as well as those of Socrates, Confucius, and Jesus, quite probably contain a certain element of fiction. But this element, if present, is designed to illustrate the ideal in human beings, and to inspire in men the courage and wisdom to attempt, insofar as they are able, to attain that ideal. And in fact, even if all elements of the fictional were to be carefully winnowed from the biographies of these men, they would still remain without doubt among the greatest figures to appear in the history of human society over the past three thousand years.

The Buddhist scriptures, the Bible, even the dialogues of Plato, are not to be judged in the same category as ordinary works of literature. They contain detailed accounts of the wisdom won through great effort and struggle by the great religious leaders of mankind, and of philosophies of life that are inexhaustible in depth and inspiration. If these works had confined themselves to a dry recital of the historical facts concerning the lives of the men whose teachings they record, one wonders if they would ever have been as widely, as fervently, and as continuously read over the centuries as they have.

In the case of Buddhism, there is one more point that must be kept in mind. As the scriptures continually remind us, the teachings of the Buddha are intended to bring salvation to all sentient beings. The early disciples, in compiling the canon, were not simply putting together a record of Shakyamuni's words and actions. They were speaking and acting in his stead. If they themselves had not been able to enter into the same lofty state of mind as the Buddha, they could not have understood Shakyamuni's teachings, nor could they have handed them down to later ages. This is why we say that each word and phrase of the sutras represents the golden sayings of the Buddha. And when we, as followers of Buddhism, stand with the scriptures in hand and challenge the society of our time, we too, like the disciples some two thousand years ago, must enter into the same state of mind as the Buddha himself. We must give ourselves wholly to the task of bringing light to the masses of men and women who are lost in suffering and of teaching them the true way of life.

2

The Theravada and
the Mahasanghika

The Background of the Second Council

A hundred years after the First Council, a second great Buddhist conclave took place, known as the Second Council. Some sources place the date at 110 years after the Buddha's death. In any event, it is from around this time that the Buddhist Order appears to have split into two major divisions, one known as the Theravada or "Teaching of the Elders," the other as the Mahasanghika or "Members of the Great Order." The Buddhism of the former was in later times transmitted to the countries south and east of India and constituted the origin of the type of Buddhism which prevails today in such countries as Sri Lanka, Thailand, Burma, Cambodia, Laos, and so on.

From this fact we may surmise that the motives which led to the calling of the Second Council were very different from those behind the First Council, when Shakyamuni's sorrowing disciples gathered together to honor him and perpetuate his memory.

We are told that Upali, who had played an important role at the First Council, died thirty years after the Buddha, and we may suppose that most of the rest of Shakyamuni's disciples died around the same time. Surely it is difficult to imagine that anyone who had known the Buddha in person could still have been alive a hundred years after his death. Thus by the time of the Second Council, the Buddhist Order, we may surmise, was headed by men who belonged to the fourth or fifth generation after that of its founder.

In those hundred years, times had undoubtedly changed considerably, as had the way of life of the people of India, and it was probably inevitable that differences should have arisen concerning the manner in which the injunctions and doctrines of Shakyamuni should be interpreted.

We know that Buddhism was gradually gaining a place of importance in Indian society and was acquiring a large number of followers among the common people. One proof of this is the fact that the Mahasanghika was said to have drawn its support largely from lay believers, an indication of the degree to which the new religion had spread among the common people. At the same time, the number of Buddhists among the rulers and nobles of the cities, as well as the merchants and artisans, also increased. Monasteries were founded in many regions, and the religion, from its base in eastern India around the kingdom of Magadha, was gradually disseminated in all directions.

It was a difference of opinion concerning the precepts that led to the convening of the Second Council. A group of monks of the Vajji tribe from the city of Vaishali, we are told, had come forward with a new interpretation of the "Ten Precepts," the basic rules of discipline for the monks of the Order, and the Council was convened to consider the validity of their interpretation.

The monks of Vaishali drew up a list of ten actions, heretofore prohibited to members of the Order, and proposed that they be declared permissible. The first item, for example, proposed that monks be allowed to store away salt; previously, the storing away of any kind of foodstuff had been prohibited. Other items would have permitted the monks to eat after the noon hour, an action normally forbidden; under certain circumstances to use bedding, mats, and robes that departed from the prescribed size; and to drink certain beverages ordinarily forbidden. The last item, which proposed that monks be allowed to accept gifts of gold and silver, was apparently the most controversial of all, since the accepting of any kind of monetary alms had been strictly forbidden in the past.

As one can see, the monks of the time lived a highly circumscribed life, one that it is difficult to imagine the Buddhist clergy of modern times, at least in Japan, being willing to tolerate. Of course if a man in the Indian society of the time made up his mind to leave ordinary life and become a monk, he must have been fully prepared to abide by the strict discipline of the Order. And yet one cannot help feeling that the kind of stern asceticism that forbids the members of the Order even to lay aside a small store of salt or demands that they receive its sanction before presuming to regulate the smallest details of their life must in the end diminish and impair the basic humanity of the persons subjected to it. In effect, it inhibits the very spirit of enterprise and activism needed to carry out the main objective of the Order, that of spreading abroad the teachings of Buddhism.

One of the reasons that the Order had fallen into this highly regulated asceticism was that the monks had come to have a strong consciousness of themselves as a special class in society. They saw themselves as a group set apart from the common run of men and carrying out special religious practices; this consciousness, we may surmise, led them to make the rules governing their lives ever more detailed and exacting. True discipline, however, should not be something imposed upon the individual from the outside. It should spring up instinctively from within him and form the basis for his dealings with the external world. This does not seem to have been the case with the early Buddhist monks. Rather it was their impulse to shut themselves off from the outside world that inspired their rules of discipline, and these rules in turn further isolated them from society as a whole.

It is important to note that the stirrings of opposition should have appeared in the city of Vaishali, the home of the famous lay believer Vimalakirti, of whom we shall have more to say later. The city was a flourishing center of free commerce and also served as the capital of the Vajji, a confederation of five tribal groups having a republican form of government headed by representatives of the tribes. In view of the relatively progressive and cosmopolitan atmosphere of the city it is quite easy to imagine a new movement arising among the members of the Buddhist community there that sought to break out of the shell of discipline-oriented isolation.

Buddhism was originally intended for all men and women in society, and should never have been allowed to become the possession of one special class. Such was the contention of the leaders of this new movement, and they called for a return to the original spirit of Buddhism as it had been propounded by Shakyamuni.

The ten precepts of the Vajji monks would have allowed them to perform certain actions hitherto prohibited to members of the Order. It was not long, however, before word of their innovations reached the more conservative elders of the Order, who greeted it with alarm. In the eyes of these older monks, themselves strict observers of the rules of discipline laid down by the First Council, the appearance of monks who willfully broke the rules constituted a threat to the Order of the utmost gravity.

Before long, a number of elder monks from all over India had assembled in a garden in the city of Vaishali to consider the problem. Five monks each were chosen as representatives of those coming from eastern and western India respectively and were charged with the task of examining the "Ten Precepts" of the Vaishali monks in the light of the teachings on discipline handed down from the First Council. After branding them as the "Ten Unlawful Things," they submitted their condemnation to the members of the gathering as a whole for formal confirmation.

When this had been done, the leader of the meeting selected seven hundred monks and had them perform a group recitation of the sutras and rules of discipline, just as Mahakashyapa had done at the time of the First Council. Thus ended the Second Council, or the "Gathering of the Seven Hundred Monks," as it is sometimes called.

The proposals of the Vajji monks were rejected in toto by the elders of the Order. I personally cannot help feeling that these demands were to some extent justified. I say this because it seems to me that the Elders, by placing all emphasis upon the omnipotence and unassailability of the rules of discipline, had departed rather far in spirit from the breadth and tolerance of Shakyamuni, who had taught men and women how to live as human beings. It would appear, therefore, that the Buddhist Order a hundred years after the death of its founder had reached the point where it was in need of reform.

As a matter of fact, we are told that Shakyamuni himself indicated that the rules governing the Order could be somewhat modified or in some cases abandoned, provided the members of the Order were in full agreement on the matter. Shakyamuni's attitude toward the rules of discipline is further indicated by the fact that (as related in my earlier volume) when the disciple Devadatta proposed the so-called Five Practices, a set of precepts which would have imposed a life of severe asceticism upon the monks, Shakyamuni rejected them outright. He was a man of great human breadth and profundity who, far from attempting to impose a fixed set of tenets or rules of discipline upon others, had a genius for adapting himself to the specific individual character of whomever he was addressing and expounding the truths of the Dharma to the person in a way that made them genuinely meaningful. He was not a disciplinarian but a true "man of freedom," an extoller of the marvelous power and vitality of the life force.

At the time of the First Council, there was considerable difference of opinion as to just how much emphasis should be placed upon the rules of discipline, and the participants could not arrive at any decision on the matter. Thereupon, according to the scriptural accounts, Mahakashyapa decreed that the precepts Shakyamuni had laid down for the Order should be abided by without the slightest deviation. As a result, it would seem that the monks became completely absorbed in the observance of the rules of discipline, and at the same time the doctrines of the new religion became fixed to the extent that freedom of interpretation was no longer regarded as permissible. This, then, was the rigid state which we find the Buddhist Order to have been in some hundred years after Shakyamuni's death.

Buddhist doctrine enunciates a principle known by the term *zuihō-bini*. According to this principle, so long as there is no violation of the main tenets and precepts of the Dharma, it is permissible to adapt to the customs and practices of the particular area in which one is preaching or living. Thus, for example, Shakyamuni is reported to have told the monks that, in the matter of diet and times of eating, they should follow the practices of the region in which they lived and need not necessarily abide by the rules he himself laid down. This may be why the "Ten Precepts" of the Vajji monks contain so many changes in matters pertaining to meals.

The Origins of the Schism

At the time we are discussing, Buddhism in India seems to have existed in the form of a number of fairly autonomous groups situated throughout the country. Partly this was the inevitable result of the difficulties of communication; it would have been all but impossible to coordinate the activities of all these far-flung groups under a single central authority. In addition, the Nirvana Sutra tells us that Shakyamuni himself said he had no intention of directing a large religious organization, and presumably from the first there was no attempt to keep the Order functioning as a single unified body. After Shakyamuni's death, therefore, we may suppose that a number of separate organizations were formed in various localities, each centered around one of the important disciples of the founder. It is not surprising, then, that a hundred years later there should have appeared subtle doctrinal and ritual differences among these various groups. Such, in any event, is the way in which most scholars of Buddhism describe the early situation of the Order.

Even as late as the seventh century A.D., when the famous Chinese Buddhist pilgrim Hsüan-tsang visited India, he found various groups devoted to the teachings of one or another of the Buddha's major disciples, such as Shariputra or Maudgalyayana. That Indian Buddhism was characterized by a number of regional organizations each having its own particular characteristics would thus appear to be a historical fact. This is hardly surprising when we consider that Shakyamuni himself made a practice of preaching the Dharma in different ways depending upon the capacity of the person or groups he was addressing to understand it.

The question of greatest concern to the student of Buddhism is whether these groups preserved the true spirit of Shakyamuni's teachings. If they remained faithful to the overall principles of his doctrine, then minor local variations in the observance of the rules of discipline could be overlooked. The Dharma clearly teaches that one must devote himself to three concerns: the observation of the precepts, the practice of *dhyana* or meditation, and the cultivation of *prajna* or wisdom. The group that in time came to be known as the Theravada or "Teaching of the Elders," however, laid stress entirely upon the rules of discipline. By contrast, the group known as the Mahasanghika or "Members of the Great Order" believed that they were carrying out the true teachings of Shakyamuni by mingling with the common mass of people, talking with them, sharing their sufferings, and encouraging them in the practice of the Buddhist faith.

We have mentioned earlier the spirit of freedom and independence that characterized the city of Vaishali, as represented by the lay believer Vimalakirti, who in the sutra that bears his name is depicted as criticizing even the Ten Major Disciples of Shakyamuni when he felt they were too stubborn or fixed in their ideas and practices. It is easy to imagine, therefore, that the monks of Vaishali should have differed from those of other regions in the manner in which they ate their meals, their attitude toward gifts of money, and other points of discipline.

In any event, the Second Council flatly rejected the proposals put forward by the Vaishali monks, who at the conclusion of the council gathered together a group of ten thousand monks and held a council of their own, referred to as the "Great Group Recitation." In time they came to be known as the Mahasanghika or "Members of the Great Order," to distinguish them from the Theravada or "Teaching of the Elders" group, and the Buddhist Order became divided into two factions. We are told that in the first hundred years there were no factions, but during the second hundred years the teaching of Shakyamuni was subject to seventeen different schools of interpretation. The beginning of the process of division took place with the schism that resulted from the Second Council.

The fact that so many different sects could have been formed in the second hundred years of Buddhism must have been a serious blow to the Theravada elders, who looked upon themselves as the leaders of the Order as a whole. Furthermore, we are told that in the following hundred years the process of division continued until there were as many as eighteen sects, twelve of them belonging to the Theravada line and six to the Mahasanghika. Chinese translations of the scriptures record an even higher number, claiming that there were twenty sects, eleven belonging to the Theravada and nine to the Mahasanghika. Whatever the exact figures may have been, there is no doubt that Buddhism had entered a period of pronounced sectarianism.

I cannot help thinking that the responsibility for this rests largely with the party of the Elders. At a later period, the followers of Mahayana Buddhism referred to the Theravada group disparagingly as the Hinayana or "Lesser Vehicle," and although it is no more than personal conjecture, I wonder if the Theravadins had not perhaps earned the epithet by forgetting the vigorously active spirit characteristic of Buddhism during the lifetime of Shakyamuni, isolating themselves from the general populace, and sinking into a petty authoritarianism. If they had not to some extent lost sight of Shakyamuni's true teachings, I do not believe that the religion would have been troubled by schism to the degree that it was.

Looking at it from another point of view, however, it is possible that this was a process that the religion was destined to go through as the Dharma, originally the possession of a single man, Shakyamuni, became the possession of millions. We may look upon this period as one of troubled and painful growth, when all conceivable interpretations were put forward, to be followed in time by a brighter one when, like a great river, the teachings would flow forth with new power and confidence.

If we examine the accounts of the Second Council, we will see that the Vajji monks in proposing their reinterpretation of the Ten Precepts did not, at least at the outset, intend to bring about a schism. The trouble began when a monk belonging to what later became the party of the "Elders" happened to be traveling through Vaishali and saw the Vajji monks accepting monetary gifts from the laity. Startled and outraged, he decided to make an issue of it.

The acceptance of gifts of money from lay believers does not by any means indicate that the Vajji monks had sunk into moral depravity. After the Second Council, as we have seen, some ten thousand of them held a meeting of their own, surely an indication that they were a large and flourishing group who enjoyed wide support among the populace at large. Possibly this very fact aroused feelings of envy among the party of the Elders.

Vaishali was a thriving center of commerce, situated as it was at a midpoint along the trade route between the city of Savatthi in the north and Rajagaya to the south, and we may suppose that the monks living there had no choice but to accept alms in the form of money. In comparison with the time of Shakyamuni, this was a period when a monetary economy was developing very rapidly in India. It was perfectly natural for the citizens of Vaishali to present alms to the monks in the form of money rather than food. From this point of view, the reinterpretation of the Ten Precepts may be seen as an attempt to adjust the rules of the Order to the new conditions prevailing in the society of the time.

The manner in which the party of the Elders dealt with the matter was, as we have seen, authoritarian and harsh in the extreme. They deliberately called together as many of the older monks as possible, set them to proving the illegality of the proposed changes, and branded them as "unlawful." Not content with that, they went a step farther, declaring that the Vajji monks who had put them forward were "not true monks or followers of Shakyamuni!"

In the view of the Elders, the Vajji monks may have appeared to be troublemakers intent upon disrupting the peace of the Order. They may have been tempted to compare them to Devadatta, the disciple who brought about a temporary schism in the Order during the time of Shakyamuni.

Actually, however, the two cases are basically quite different. Devadatta, it appears, had ambitions to replace Shakyamuni as leader of the Order. The "Five Practices" which he proposed would have imposed a more severe asceticism upon the monks, and his aim in making the proposal was apparently to impress the younger monks with his piety and gain their support so that he could set himself up as a new Buddha at the head of an organization of his own. He deliberately sought to create a schism and was indeed a disrupter of the peace.

The Vajji monks, on the other hand, had no intention of creating division in the Order. Rather they were attempting to adjust the rules to local customs and the changed conditions of society, as Shakyamuni had indicated should be done, pursuing their own particular religious practices in the spirit of the Buddhism originally taught by Shakyamuni. The Elders, in choosing to make an issue of the matter, magnified it to the point where it precipitated a split in the Order.

The Elders' dogmatic attitude is reflected in the later writings of the Theravada sect. There the Great Group Recitation of the Mahasanghika monks is described in the following words: "The monks of the Great Group Recitation settled upon doctrines that are at variance with the true Dharma. They destroyed the original records and made up records of their own. They took sutras that were recorded in one place in the canon and moved them to another place . . . they discarded a portion of the most profound sutras and precepts and made up sutras and precepts that resembled them or in some cases were entirely different . . . They discarded the rules that govern nouns, gender, phraseology, and stylistic embellishment and substituted different ones."

In spite of these drastic charges, an examination of the extant texts, as pointed out by the Buddhist scholar Fumio Masutani, suggests that there was no basic difference in the writings and doctrines of the two groups. That is to say, the scriptures of both the Theravada and Mahasanghika sects follow the same four-part arrangement found in the older *Agama* sutras. Certainly there was no such major difference as was later to characterize the Mahayana and Hinayana divisions of Buddhism.

There is one important point to note regarding this first major schism in early Buddhism. The accounts of the break, particularly the one quoted above, suggest that we have here the kind of situation so often described in Western religious history as a confrontation between "dogmatism and revisionism" or between "orthodoxy and heterodoxy." Such terminology, however, is in my opinion not necessarily apt. In Western Christianity, with its heresy trials and witch hunts, once a schism had developed, the two sides not infrequently fell upon one another in violence and bloodshed, using every means available to wipe out the opponent. But in the case of Buddhism, although the Theravada and Mahasanghika groups parted company after the Second Council, neither made any attempt to harass the other, much less did they resort to violence. This is indicative of the essential spirit of tolerance and respect for human life that characterizes Buddhism.

On the surface, the Theravada monks would appear to be the upholders of orthodoxy and the Mahasanghika monks the heretics. And yet if we are to employ terms like these, we must consider which group was in fact abiding more faithfully by the original spirit of Buddhism. Not those who held themselves aloof from society but those who plunged in among the mass of men and women, enduring their hardships in an effort to save as many as possible, are surely the ones who deserve to be called the true defenders of orthodoxy.

Again, in ordinary terms the Theravada monks would seem to be the dogmatists and the Mahasanghika monks the revisionists. But again we must ask which group was acting more nearly in the spirit of Shakyamuni. Was *he* in fact a hidebound dogmatist? Or, for that matter, was he the kind of revisionist who is willing to sacrifice any principle for the sake of compromise? Was he not in fact a proponent of the middle way, transcending the kind of dualism represented by such terms as *dogmatist* and *revisionist*? This middle way constituted the essence of the Truth which he preached. From this point of view it is apparent that to quibble over minor details concerning the rules of discipline or to engage with others in an argument over who is the true upholder of orthodoxy is an act far removed from the original spirit of Buddhism.

The Movement to Restore the Original Meaning of Buddhism

As we have seen, the break between the Theravada and the Mahasanghika groups came about not only because of differences over the rules of discipline, but also because the former had become an isolated body that placed all emphasis upon the monastic life. As Teruhiro Watanabe and other scholars have pointed out, the religious groups associated with the Theravada lineage stressed monasticism and withdrawal from ordinary life and were tradition-bound and elitist in outlook. The monks of the Mahasanghika lineage, on the other hand, emphasized the importance of work among the masses, even though it might mean sacrificing one's own chances for achieving enlightenment. The latter outlook in time led to the great movement known as Mahayana Buddhism, but presages of what was to come were apparently already present in the directions in which the Mahasanghika monks were moving. It was this basic difference of outlook that led to the rift between the two groups rather than the rather superficial dispute over the interpretation of the Ten Precepts.

The Mahayana scriptures thoroughly condemn the so-called *shōmon* or *shravakas*, persons who exert themselves to attain the stage of arhat, and the *engaku* or *pratyeka-buddhas*, persons who strive only for their own enlightenment, these censures presumably being aimed at the isolation and withdrawal from the world that marked the Theravada monks. Among such monastic groups, it was the length of time one had been a monk or the number of sutras and precepts one could recite from memory that determined whether one merited the title of arhat or saint.

In contrast with this kind of monasticism, the Mahayana scriptures stress the concept of the *bosatsu* or bodhisattva, the believer who works not only for "self profit," that is, for the attainment of his own enlightenment, but for the "profit of others," actively seeking to spread the teachings of the faith among the populace at large.

The evidence indicates that the monks of the Theravada lineage at the time we are discussing had become highly conservative. Although in the literal sense one may attempt to *conserve* the teachings of Shakyamuni by shutting oneself off from society, this does nothing to help spread and promote the growth of the Dharma. A religion that isolates itself in this fashion will soon find itself at an impasse, and in fact the Dharma itself can no longer continue to exist among men who attempt to remove themselves from the pains, sufferings and mortal limitations of their fellow human beings or persistently ignore them. Therefore it is only natural that the monks of the Mahasanghika, who enjoyed wide popular support,

37

should have appeared with their new proposals in an effort to break through the impasse.

It is well to remember that Shakyamuni himself did not spend all his time preaching to the monks alone. Though obliged each year to go into retirement during the rainy season, he spent the greater part of his lifetime working to spread his teachings among the populace in general so that all men might gain enlightenment. If Shakyamuni's preachings had been intended only for the members of the monastic order, then Buddhism would never have become a major world religion.

Already in Shakyamuni's lifetime the monks, after they had received a certain amount of training under him, customarily dispersed to various localities to devote themselves to preaching activities there. To take one example, Purna, one of the Buddha's major disciples, who came from a town on the western coast of India, received permission from Shakyamuni to return to his native region, where he dedicated the remainder of his life to the spreading of the faith. For this reason, he was not able to be present at the death of the Buddha or the First Council. One source goes so far as to state that when he returned east to the city of Rajagaha at a later date and was pressed by the members of the Order there to give his sanction to the version of the canon as it had been fixed at the First Council, he refused to do so.

In this connection there is a very interesting legend reported by the Chinese monk Hsüan-tsang, which he heard on his visit to India in the middle of the seventh century. According to this, there were actually two groups gathered together at the time of the First Council. The first, consisting of five hundred elder monks headed by Mahakashyapa, met within the cave of Saptaparna and compiled one version of the canon. But there was also a second group of monks who gathered "outside the cave" and compiled their own version of the canon. The elder monks, as we have seen, concentrated their attention upon the rules of discipline, while the canon compiled by the group outside the cave reflected dissatisfaction with this narrow focus of interest and served as the basis of what in later times was to become the Mahasanghika school of thought.

This suggests that the first canon, because it was drawn up primarily to meet the needs of the monastic community, was difficult for those members of the Order who intended to live and work among the populace to accept. Thus we may surmise that the conditions that were later to bring about the compilation of the Mahayana scriptures were already to some extent in existence at the time of the First Council.

Different standards and rules of discipline were obviously needed for different groups within the Buddhist community. It was the duty of the monks to preserve and hand on correctly the teachings of the faith, and in exchange for discharging this duty they were supported by the alms of the laity. It is only natural, therefore, for the lay believers to expect the monks to observe strict rules of discipline and to devote all their energies to religious practice.

On the other hand, there was no need for the laymen to conform to such difficult codes of behavior. Of course there were certain duties as Buddhist believers and members of society that they had to fulfill, but these were in no way as exacting as the elaborate precepts laid down for the monks. This too was undoubtedly one of the factors leading to the subtle differences in outlook that characterized the Theravada school, centered about the monastic community, and the Mahasanghika, which maintained close contact with the lay community.

Not only the rules of discipline to be observed but the manner in which the teachings of the Buddha were understood differed somewhat between the monks and the lay believers. The so-called *shōmon* were those disciples who had the opportunity to listen in person to the Buddha's preachings and devoted themselves constantly to the perfecting of their own understanding and character. After the death of the Buddha, they presumably continued to study under those elder monks who had received the Dharma directly from the Buddha. For such men, the number of sutras and precepts they could recite from memory was an indication of how far they had progressed in their religious training.

For the general lay believer, a mere phrase or word of the Buddha might be the means to salvation. Even during Shakyamuni's lifetime, there must have been numerous laymen who had never received instruction directly from the Buddha but who nevertheless made his teachings, as transmitted to them by others, the sole support of their lives. The question was not how many sutras they were familiar with, but how well they preserved and perfected the spirit of the Dharma in their daily lives.

Shakyamuni, knowing how grave the responsibility of the monastic order would be in preserving and spreading his teachings after his death, no doubt made the rules of discipline for the monks purposely strict. But in the years following his death, they seem to have lost sight of the fact that the rules of discipline were merely a means to insure the health of the Order and not an end in themselves. Instead of going out among the masses to spread the message of Buddhism, they withdrew from society and concentrated entirely upon their own enlightenment and religious practice. It was this unfortunate situation that gave rise to the appearance of the Mahasanghika movement.

This movement may be described as an effort to return to the original meaning of Buddhism as Shakyamuni had expounded it. As I have stressed earlier, the break between the Theravada and the Mahasanghika should not be interpreted in terms of a struggle between orthodoxy and heterodoxy. In Buddhism all reform movements have as their starting point this spirit of striving to return to the fundamentals of the faith. Such movements begin as a small minority within the religion as a whole, but if they are successful in their attempt to reestablish the fundamental principles of the doctrine, they will in time gain in force until they have become the majority. The fate of Buddhism rests upon the ability to recapture these fundamentals and to apply them correctly in practice.

What was Shakyamuni's purpose in devoting fifty years of his life to the preaching of the Dharma? It was to bring salvation to all men and women and to release them from the sufferings of birth, old age, sickness, and death. A monk, never forgetting this fundamental fact, must be determined to sacrifice his own being for the welfare of mankind. This is the spirit which, as we shall see, later found expression in Mahayana Buddhism.

3

King Ashoka

The King of Monarchs

The third century B.C. in India saw the appearance of King Ashoka, who played a crucial role in the spread of Buddhism. The Mauryan empire, which Ashoka ruled, held domain over all except the southern tip of India, and extended its influence south into Sri Lanka and west into the territory of the Greek states, regions into which Buddhism was introduced. We are told that in Ashoka's reign, Buddhist monks journeyed from India to the Greek states, spreading a knowledge of their religion, winning seventy-three thousand converts, and ordaining one thousand monks.

The name of Ashoka brings to mind the following anecdote recorded in a Buddhist work. According to the account, Shakyamuni was once going about begging in the outskirts of the city of Rajagaha when he came upon two little boys playing in the sand. The boys, observing the so-called "thirty-two distinguishing features of a great man" that the Buddha was said to have possessed, decided that they should make an offering to him and proceeded to mold the sand into cakes and place them in Shakyamuni's begging bowl. One of them then pressed his palms together in a gesture of reverence. Shakyamuni received the gift of sand cakes with a smile. The disciple Ananda, who was accompanying him, asked him why he smiled, whereupon he replied, "I have a reason for smiling, Ananda, and you shall know it. One hundred years after my death, this boy will become a Chakravarti king at Pataliputra who will rule over all regions. His name will be Ashoka, and he will rule through the true Dharma. In addition, he will distribute my relics abroad, will build eighty-four thousand stupas in honor of the King of the

Dharma, and will bring comfort to countless living beings."

The point of the anecdote, of course, is to emphasize that in the giving of alms it is not the nature of the gift but the spirit in which it is offered that is important. The children presented their sand cakes in a spirit of innocence and purity of heart, and the Buddha accepted them with gratitude. Unfortunately, adults too often adopt a calculating attitude when making offerings, thereby canceling the merit that might otherwise be gained if the gift had been given in a spirit of true generosity and reverence.

Western scholars, with their customary skepticism, long regarded Ashoka as a legendary figure who existed only in the writings of the Buddhists. But in 1837 the earliest Indian inscriptions were finally deciphered, and as more and more edicts inscribed by Ashoka on rocks and pillars came to light through excavation, it became evident that he was not only a historical figure but, as H. G. Wells said of him, was in fact "one of the greatest rulers the world has ever seen." The reason for the high praise heaped upon him lies in his having been the first monarch to abandon warfare, to adopt a policy of absolute pacifism based upon the ideals of Buddhism, and to take vigorous steps to insure the health and welfare of his subjects. Count Coudenhove-Kalergi, a proponent of European unity, once remarked to me in conversation that he regarded Ashoka as "deserving of high respect among all the rulers of world history," and the English biologist J. B. S. Haldane also observed that he wished he had been born in the age of Ashoka.

It is the peace and humanitarianism of his rule, of course, that have inspired these Westerners to expressions of admiration, hardly surprising when one recalls the almost incessant warfare that has characterized European history. It is easy enough to expound a policy of peace, but very few leaders in the history of mankind have actually applied such a policy. Yet Ashoka, living over two thousand years ago in India, demonstrated that it is possible to put one's ideals of pacifism into action. Moreover, as a Buddhist believer himself, he outlawed the killing of living creatures and took measures to ensure the welfare of his people, such as planting trees along the roads, digging wells at intervals, setting up rest houses for travelers, and supplying herbs and medicines to his subjects. He played an extremely important role in propagating Buddhism and helping to make it one of the world's major religions, and for this reason he deserves to be carefully studied.

In a sense Ashokan studies are still in their infancy. Until 1915 he was not even looked upon as a historical personage. It is quite possible that further excavations may bring to light more of his inscriptions, and we may come to learn even more about this remarkable figure.

King Ashoka seems to have come to the throne around 268 B.C. According to the Sanskrit Buddhist canon, this was just a hundred years after the death of Shakyamuni, while according to works of the Pali canon, it was 218 years after Shakyamuni's death. These figures, in fact, are among the most important data employed by scholars in attempting to establish the date of the Buddha's death, but this is a problem too complex to go into here.

Seven years after he ascended the throne, Ashoka embraced Buddhism, becoming an *upasaka* or male lay believer, though at first he does not seem to have been very fervent in his faith. In the ninth year of his reign, he attacked the state of Kalinga, in the region of present day Orissa, killing some one hundred thousand persons and capturing and transferring to other regions one hundred fifty thousand more. At this time he apparently underwent a change of heart. According to one inscription, the sight of the suffering and death grieved him deeply, and he vowed never again to go to war.

Before that expedition, he is said to have been referred to widely as "Ashoka the tyrant." According to legend, at the time he came to the throne he murdered ninety-nine of his male relatives, and after his enthronement did away with five hundred high officials. After the attack on Kalinga, he abandoned a rule based upon military force for one based upon the Dharma and henceforward became known as "Ashoka of the Dharma."

Though one may speak of "rule based upon the Dharma," it must have been a very difficult ideal for Ashoka to realize. Even after his conquest of Kalinga, there were many wild tribes living in the hills and forests along the borders of his empire who posed an ever present threat to peace, while we may be certain that the Brahmans and other groups in society who opposed his rule were constantly watching for an opportunity to trip him up. According to one source, there were at this time 118 different tribes living in various parts of India, and northwest India in particular was the scene of constant strife. Though the Mauryan kings had succeeded in uniting almost all of the subcontinent under their rule, Ashoka's position was by no means a completely peaceful and stable one. The Buddhist texts indicate that he faced danger any number of times during his long rule.

The Mauryan dynasty was founded by Chandragupta, Ashoka's grandfather and an ardent follower of the Jain faith, through the use of military force. In 327 B.C. Alexander the Great had invaded India, but after his retreat, Chandragupta succeeded in driving out the Greek garrisons and around 317 B.C. attacked and overthrew the ruler of the Nanda kingdom to establish the first unified empire in Indian history.

Chandragupta, with the aid of a wily minister named Kautilya, set up a network of political spies throughout the empire and ruled largely through terror. In 305 B.C. he engaged in battle with Seleucus Nicator, the Greek king of Syria, and seems to have gotten the better of him. A peace alliance was arranged whereby Chandragupta received a daughter of the Syrian king as his wife.

Chandragupta's son Bindusara succeeded him as ruler and appears to have carried on the stern administrative measures devised for his father by Kautilya. He is noteworthy for having had sixteen wives, and as a result Ashoka was said to have had a total of 101 brothers and sisters. Bindusara was a typical example of the so-called Oriental despot, and it is only reasonable to suppose that he faced constant threats to his position both from within the country and from abroad.

The same was true, as we have seen, of Ashoka. Greek legend speaks of the "sword of Damocles," and Ashoka too must often have felt himself to be in the same perilous position, never knowing when or from what quarter an attempt would be launched to overthrow him. Such is the fate of the powerful.

In Ashoka's case, however, the horrors he witnessed at Kalinga revealed to him the frightful nature of existence. He himself states in one of his edicts that two years and a half after becoming an *upasaka* and over one year after associating closely with the Buddhist Order and engaging ardently in religious practice, he has become increasingly confident that he can rule through the Dharma. And in fact, as we have seen, he went on to become the greatest monarch in all of Indian history. It is for this reason that the state of India today has chosen as the design for its official seal the lion-crowned capital of one of the pillars erected by King Ashoka.

Nevertheless, the praise and glory that Ashoka has enjoyed down through the long centuries of history are by no means due to his own personal power and ability as a ruler. Rather they are to be regarded as the fruits of those doctrines first implanted in the Indian soil by Shakyamuni and carefully nourished and protected by the numberless followers of the early Buddhist Order.

Absolute Pacifism in Government

Let us examine some of the edicts inscribed by King Ashoka on rocks and pillars and see just how his government functioned. The Thirteenth Rock Edict, after describing his conquest of the state of Kalinga and the sufferings witnessed at that time, then goes on to say: "But there is something that I, the Beloved of the Gods, find even more grievous: that all the inhabitants—Brahmans, ascetics, and other sectarians, and householders who are obedient to superiors, parents, and elders, who treat friends, acquaintances, companions, relatives, slaves, and servants with respect, and are firm in their faith—all suffer violence, murder, and separation from their loved ones."

After expressing compassion for the sufferings of his people, he declares that the highest form of conquest is the conquest that is carried out through the Dharma, and he vows to cherish and take delight in the Dharma and to work to spread it abroad. He also indicates that by sending envoys he has called upon various states on the borders of his empire to renounce warfare and join with him in peace and friendship.

Specifically, we are told in this and another edict, he dispatched envoys southward to the lands of the Cholas, Pandyas, Satyaputras, Keralaputras, and the island of Sri Lanka, and westward to five Greek kings, Antiochus II Theos of Syria, Ptolemy II Philadelphus of Egypt, Antigonus Gonatas of Macedonia, Magas of Cyrene, and Alexander II of Epirus (or perhaps Alexander of Corinth).

It is little wonder that Western scholars have been moved to admiration by the vigor of King Ashoka's labors to carry out his policy of peaceful diplomacy. Mankind in the latter part of the twentieth century is just now beginning to try to work out some kind of machinery to insure peaceful coexistence among nations, though the major powers continue to build up vast stores of armaments and to negotiate with one another in a spirit of secrecy and mutual suspicion. King Ashoka, by contrast, appealed for absolute pacifism based upon the ideals of Buddhism, and unilaterally proclaimed that he was renouncing warfare, a step that is extremely difficult for a large nation to take. The Japanese Constitution is rare among the constitutions of the world in its renunciation of war, and yet Japan today ranks seventh in the world in terms of military power. This seems to me an indication that Japan still has a long way to go in understanding and embracing the ideal of absolute pacifism.

According to the accounts, King Ashoka, once he had determined to rule by means of the Dharma, reduced his armaments and employed his troops solely for parades or ceremonial occasions. The records likewise indicate that the farmers and other groups in society were no longer required to perform military service. Thus his rule of the Dharma was not forced upon the people by a highly militarized state.

Ashoka's policy, even when dealing with the recalcitrant tribes along the border, was to treat his subjects as he would his own children. This spirit is clearly brought out in the following edict, which was addressed to the officials who were being sent to the newly conquered state of Kalinga. The edict reads in part as follows:

"All men are my children, and as I wish all welfare and happiness in this world and the next for my own children, so do I wish it for all men. But I believe that among the various border peoples who have not yet submitted there are those who think to themselves, 'What does the King want with us?' I will then tell you in truth the only thing that I want with the border peoples. 'This is what the King wants: I want the border peoples to be free from fear because of me, I want them to trust me, and to receive only comfort from my hands and not to receive hardship from me.' They should be made to understand this. They should also be made to understand this: 'The King endures all that he is able to endure for their sake. And if they will abide by my teachings and practice the Dharma, they will surely obtain welfare and happiness in this world and the next.' "

The phrase "all men are my children" is particularly striking, a vivid expression of the Buddhist doctrine of the equality of all men, regardless of which of the four traditional classes of Indian society they might belong to. Buddhism also teaches that one is indebted to all living beings, and it would appear that King Ashoka too recognized such an obligation toward all the living things, not only within his kingdom but throughout the whole world. One wonders how many such rulers have appeared in the course of history.

In east or west, past or present, the great majority of men in power seem concerned only with imposing their will upon the people under them by whatever forceful measures may be needed. Those who recognize that they also have obligations to their people are few indeed.

Ashoka's determination to rule as righteously and effectively as possible is evident from the Sixth Rock Edict, which reads in part as follows:

"For a long time in the past no ruler has been willing to decide on affairs of state or listen to petitions at any hour of the day. But I now issue the following command. Whether I am at my meals, or in the women's quarters, or in my chamber, or in my menagerie, or riding in a chariot, or in my pleasure gardens, officials with petitions to present to me concerning the governing of the people shall be allowed to present them at any time and any place. If they do so, I shall in turn decide upon affairs concerning the people wherever I may happen to be. Any time a dispute shall arise in the council or a movement for revision concerning gifts or favors I have bestowed or orders which I have personally given concerning the carrying out of the edicts, or concerning the handling of grave matters that have been entrusted to the high officials, word of it shall be brought to me immediately, regardless of where I am or what time it may be."

As is clear from this edict, King Ashoka was well aware of the historical significance that attached to his methods of governing in person. He is in effect proclaiming himself to be the first monarch in history to rule not by military force but by the power of the Dharma.

It may be of interest here to note in outline the gist of the various edicts:

First Edict: prohibition of the taking of life and animal sacrifice.

Second: establishment of two types of hospitals, for men and animals, growing of herbs, planting of trees along the highways, digging of wells.

Third Edict: order concerning inspection tour of provinces to be made every five years.

47

Fourth Edict: description of measures to be taken to promulgate the Dharma.

Fifth Edict: establishment of "Dharma Officials" to implement the new policies.

Sixth Edict: order concerning speedy submission of petitions and disposal of affairs of state.

Seventh Edict: desire that all religious sects shall dwell in all regions, call for self-denial and purity of heart.

Eighth Edict: abandonment of the type of pleasure excursions indulged in by kings of the past, beginning of Dharma excursions.

Ninth Edict: prayers for the Dharma and explanation of their merits.

Tenth Edict: explanation of the fame and glory to be gained by compliance with and practice of the Dharma.

Eleventh Edict: explanation of the bestowal of the Dharma; goodwill in the name of the Dharma, sharing of goods in the name of the Dharma, and the establishment of bonds with the Dharma constitute the highest form of alms.

Twelfth Edict: call for mutual tolerance among all religious sects, statement that the nourishing of the essentials of each sect is the highest form of alms and reverence; appointment of Dharma officials, minister in charge of women, director of animal sanctuary.

Thirteenth Edict: description of horrors of the conquest of Kalinga, expression of repentance, reverence for the Dharma and determination to spread it; conquest through the Dharma declared to be highest form of conquest; envoys dispatched to states surrounding the empire, five Greek kings mentioned by name.

Fourteenth Edict: concluding words; inscriptions of edicts set up in different parts of the empire to be of three kinds: brief, fairly detailed, and very detailed, depending upon location.

In addition to these fourteen major edicts, other proclamations of King Ashoka have been found carved on smaller rocks, stone pillars of various sizes, caves, and in other forms in every part of India that was ruled by the Mauryan dynasty.

In an age that lacked our modern means of communication, it was the practice for the government to make known its aims and policies to the people by inscribing them on rocks and pillars. Though written over two thousand years ago, these words of

Ashoka seem to speak urgently to the men of today. That so many of the political leaders of the present day world lack the stature of that great monarch of antiquity is only to be regretted.

Relations between the State and Religion

Having seen how Buddhist concepts played a vital role in shaping Ashoka's ideals of benevolent government, I would like now to examine for a moment the religious situation in India in Ashoka's time.

The first important point to note is that, although Ashoka himself was an ardent Buddhist, he made no attempt to suppress other religious groups. On the contrary, he lent them positive aid and encouragement.

Ashoka was attracted to Buddhism by the teachings of the monks of Magadha. As pointed out by the Indologist D. D. Kosambi, his conversion has often been compared to the conversion of the Roman emperor Constantine to Christianity in 325. However, whereas Constantine made Christianity the official doctrine of the state and took active measures to wipe out all other religions within the Roman empire, Ashoka and his successors showed themselves to be far more tolerant, actually bestowing gifts and honors upon the Brahmans, Jains, Ajivikas, and other non-Buddhist sects. He employed Brahmans in his administration, and in his edicts expressed great respect for the other religions as well as for Buddhism.

This brings us to the question of what the proper relationship between religion and the state ought to be. The concept of the unity of Church and State is a typically Western one traceable to the early alliance between Christianity and the Roman emperors. Buddhism has always taken the attitude that the universal principles that derive from its insights as a religion should be reflected in the manner of government prevailing at the time. But this is very different from viewing religion and state as one and inseparable, and should not be confused with the latter concept.

In Ashoka's case it is clear that, as the head of a great state, he attempted to base his actions upon the Buddhist spirit of compassion and to translate that spirit into material terms through his governmental policies. In doing so, he did not attempt to impose Buddhist ideals upon the populace as religious dogma that they were required to embrace. Instead he presented these ideals as the Dharma, the Truth or way of Righteousness that all men, simply by the fact of their humanity, could understand and assent to. The key concepts of the Dharma as it was expressed in his policies were, as we have seen, the universal ideals of absolute pacificism and respect for life, ideals equally acceptable to Buddhists and non-Buddhists alike. If Ashoka had attempted to go beyond this point, declaring Buddhism the official religion of the state and taking measures to suppress Brahmanism and the other sects, he would undoubtedly have aroused the enmity of the populace and would in fact have been departing from the true spirit of Buddhism.

In this connection it is important to note the following point. Though one may argue, as is commonly done these days, that government and religion belong to essentially different orders of existence and that a monarch or government leader in his public life should treat all religions as equal, this does not mean that the head of a state is forbidden to embrace a particular religion. To establish such a prohibition would be to deprive him of "freedom of faith," which is among the generally recognized rights of the citizens in most countries today. On the contrary, a political leader with no religious faith at all would inspire mistrust and anxiety among the citizenry, making them feel like passengers in a ship whose captain has no compass. It is only when a political leader, because of his personal convictions, takes advantage of the public power at his disposal to interfere in religious affairs that difficulties arise. At such times, it becomes necessary for the populace, in order to protect their own freedom of religion, to band together and work to put an end to such political interference.

There are indications that King Ashoka, before his conversion to Buddhism, actively persecuted the monks and lay members of the Buddhist Order. It was partly for this reason that he was known as "Ashoka the tyrant." As mentioned in a number of Buddhist texts, the Buddhists took the lead in admonishing him for his ways, though they were aware that they were courting death in doing so, and in time they succeeded in making him a convert.

This process is vividly described in the Fourth Minor Rock Edict as follows:

"Ten years after my coronation, I, the Beloved of the Gods, began to preach the Dharma to my people. Since then, I have worked to nourish and spread the Dharma among the people. Thus all beings in all regions have gained happiness and well-being. As King, I have endeavored to prevent injury to living creatures and have given up the large numbers of hunters, fishermen, and hunts that other rulers have had. If anyone was intemperate in taking the life of living creatures, he has now, insofar as he is able, given up such intemperance. Thus men are obedient to their fathers and mothers and teachers, and both in this world and the next, they will be able to live along with all others in happiness and well-being."

As this and other passages in Ashoka's edicts indicate, his government was characterized by an attitude of compassion toward all forms of life. He not only called for an end to animal sacrifice and other types of killing, but he strictly practiced vegetarianism himself and for a time did not allow meat of any kind to be eaten within the palace.

We have noted above that in public life he was careful to treat all religious sects equally, even donating cave monasteries to the Ajivikas, a sect deriving from one of the so-called six unorthodox teachers described in my earlier volume and one of the chief rivals of Buddhism. But in private life he made it clear that he was a follower of the true teachings of Buddhism. Ten years after coming to the throne, he made a pilgrimage to Gaya, the place where the Buddha attained enlightenment, and thereafter, in place of the pleasure trips of his earlier days, he went on tours to inspect conditions among the people and to give them instruction, which he called "Dharma-teaching trips." He also visited Lumbini, Shakyamuni's birthplace, to pay homage, and took steps to reduce the taxes there.

Tradition tells us that he erected eighty-four thousand large temples and eighty-four thousand stupas to enshrine the relics of the Buddha, and the very large number of stupas discovered in recent years in all parts of India would seem to lend support at least to the latter assertion. These stupas also include a great many contributed by common people, thus proving beyond any possible doubt that by this time Buddhism had spread throughout all parts of India. Earlier, as we have seen, Buddhism existed in various centers scattered here and there about the country. In Ashoka's reign it for the first time became one of the national religions of India.

Ashoka also dispatched parties of Buddhist monks to various regions to help propagate the faith. One such mission, headed by Prince Mahinda, journeyed to the island of Sri Lanka and is said to have been the source of the Theravada Buddhism prevalent to this day in that country and in many of the countries of southeast Asia.

There are reported to have been sixty thousand monks residing in Pataliputra, Ashoka's capital, and we may be sure that Buddhism had entered upon a period of great flourishing and splendor. We are even told that the Brahman priests, no longer able to make a living, considered converting en masse to the Buddhist religion, though this would appear to be either an exaggeration or someone's attempt at humor.

The texts of the Pali canon report that, because the number of Buddhists was increasing at such a rapid rate and because there was fear that the teachings of the faith might become distorted or misinterpreted in the confusion, a gathering of one thousand monks was convened in Pataliputra just 236 years after the death of Shakyamuni for the purpose of putting the sacred scripture in order. It is commonly referred to as the Third Council or the Council of the Thousand Monks. Certainly it would appear that around this time the teachings of Shakyamuni were subject to a process of review and regularization and that the huge number of texts that have been handed down to today assumed something like the form they were later to have.

King Ashoka reigned for a total of thirty-seven years. During the latter twenty years or so, after the conquest of Kalinga, there was no warfare to speak of within the empire, and the people were able to enjoy a life of peace. In his Fifth Pillar Edict, Ashoka states that up to the twenty-sixth year of his reign he had ordered the release of men in prison a total of twenty-five times. In the world of the third century B.C., such humanitarianism was little short of epochal.

His existence typifies the exact antithesis of the despot who exploits and lords it over his people. We are told that he did not like to refer to himself by the customary titles of "Great King" or "Emperor" but preferred always to think of himself simply as the "king of Magadha," a further indication of how far removed he was from the usual vainglorious monarch. And it is clear that, so long as there remained any resources within the royal treasury, he devoted all his effort to improving the welfare of society.

I believe the time will come when Ashoka will be studied intensively throughout the world and his true greatness will become universally known and appreciated. I say this because so many people, faced with the crises of our modern age, are beginning to turn their eyes toward the Buddhist ideals and principles through which he ruled.

4

Questions of King Milinda

A Greek Philosopher-King

After the death of King Ashoka, the Mauryan dynasty came to an end and its vast empire was torn apart by internal dissension and invasion from abroad. Northwest India at this time came under the rule of Greek kings from Western Asia. One of the most important of these was King Menander, who ruled in the second half of the second century B.C. and who is mentioned in Indian sources. Since he had very close connections with Buddhism and represents an important point of contact between it and the world of Greek culture, I would like to discuss him here in some detail.

As we have seen, King Ashoka had earlier attempted to make known his beliefs and ideals as a Buddhist ruler to a number of Greek kings to the west of him by sending envoys to their courts. But we have no way of knowing how successful such efforts may have been, since there is no reference to his embassies in any classical Western source.

When Ashoka reigned, India was a great unified empire, clearly superior in size and might to the Greek kingdoms. By the time of King Menander, the situation was reversed. Superiority in political and military power rested with the West, and India, weak and disunified, was the victim of invasion and subjugation. And yet in matters of culture and of the spirit, East and West confronted one another as equals.

King Menander figures very importantly in a Buddhist work written in Pali and entitled *Milindapanha* or the *Questions of King Milinda*. Milinda is the Pali form of his name, and since I base my discussion on the Pali text, I shall refer to him as Milinda.

First let us see what kind of person he was. The text describes him in these words: "Milinda [was] learned, eloquent, wise, and able; and a faithful observer, and that at the right time, of all the various acts of devotion and ceremony enjoined by his own sacred hymns concerning things past, present, and to come. Many were the arts and sciences he knew — holy tradition and secular law; the Sankhya, Yoga, Nyaya, and Vaisheshika systems of philosophy; arithmetic; music; medicine; the four Vedas, the Puranas, and the Itihasas; astronomy, magic, causation, and spells; the art of war; poetry; conveyancing — in a word, the whole nineteen.

"As a disputant he was hard to equal, harder still to overcome; the acknowledged superior of all the founders of the various schools of thought. And as in wisdom so in strength of body, swiftness, and valour there was found none equal to Milinda in all India. He was rich too, mighty in wealth and prosperity, and the number of his armed hosts knew no end."[1]

This passage was probably added to the text at a later date, and we have no way to determine how accurate a portrait it represents of this ruler who lived over two thousand years ago. But it does at least indicate the degree to which learning flourished in India at this time and the large number of disciplines available for study.

In connection with arithmetic, it is interesting to note that the figures we use today are known as Arabic numerals (because they reached Europe by way of the Arabs), but they are in fact the invention of the Indians. The concept of zero was already in existence in India around two thousand years ago, though the Mayans in Central America are said to have employed it at an even earlier date. There is no doubt that Indian society at the time of King Milinda was marked by a very high level of learning and culture.

It would appear that King Milinda, in addition to receiving instruction in traditional Greek culture and learning, had also taken steps to familiarize himself with the culture and learning of India. Such a combination of Eastern and Western erudition must have made him a very awesome figure in the eyes of the ordinary Indian people. We are also told that a number of Indian philosophers engaged with him in debate, but all found themselves outwitted.

1. *The Questions of King Milinda*, T. W. Rhys Davids, tr., Part 1, pp. 6–7 (Sacred Books of the East, Vol. XXXV, Oxford: Clarendon Press, 1890; reprinted by Dover Publications, New York, 1963).

As was the custom with the Greek kings, he issued coins bearing his portrait; from photographs of them, we may see that, although not a particularly handsome man, he had an extremely intelligent face.

What motives impelled this man to take active steps to engage in debate with Indian philosophers and religious leaders of the Brahman and Buddhist faiths? Some scholars suggest that it was done purely for political reasons, in hopes of learning how to function more effectively as the ruler of an alien people. Others point out that it had been the custom from the time of Alexander the Great for Greek kings to seek instruction from the wise men of other lands. My own guess is that he was attempting to put into practice Plato's ideal of the philosopher-king, or perhaps was deliberately imitating Alexander the Great, who, it will be recalled, had studied philosophy under Aristotle.

In any event, when we examine King Milinda's methods of debate, we find them highly reminiscent of Greek philosophy. Though he may have studied Indian learning as well, his basic manner of thinking and the spirit of his approach is typically Greek. This is seen in the fact that so many of his questions are based upon an either/or pattern; that is, he presents two premises and asks which is correct. This type of approach is characteristic of Greek thought, and indeed of Western thought in general. In addition, we may note that many of the questions are deliberately designed to trip up his opponent, or are of such nature that it would be difficult to perceive what practical benefit one could gain from being able to answer them.

For example, we are told that King Milinda went to visit the antinomian philosopher Purana Kassapa and engaged in the following exchange:

" 'Who is it, venerable Kassapa, who rules the world?'

" 'The Earth, great king, rules the world!'

" 'But, venerable Kassapa, if it be the Earth that rules the world, how comes it that some men go to the Avici hell, thus getting outside the sphere of the Earth?' " [2]

Kassapa, unable to think of any way to answer, is said to have merely hung his head in silence.

Like so many people who are enchanted with their own intel-

2. *Ibid*, p. 7.

lectual powers, Milinda no doubt derived a certain pleasure from besting his opponent in this fashion. Also, we may well imagine that the Indians, though in political subjugation to the Greeks, prided themselves on being superior to the Greeks in scholarly and spiritual matters, and King Milinda therefore welcomed the opportunity to tweak their noses.

However that may be, we cannot help noting that the question is a rather foolish one, and it is difficult to understand how Purana Kassapa could possibly have been at a loss for an answer. If he had pointed out that after death creatures do not go to the Avichi Hell in their physical form, he could have gotten around the difficulty without any trouble. Or better still, he could have explained that although the Avichi Hell is said to be the lowest and hottest of the hells at the bottom of the world of desire, it is in fact nothing more than a symbol or metaphor for a state of unrelieved suffering. The king, by assuming that it literally exists somewhere outside the earth and asking how one gets there, is in reality the foolish one.

But perhaps we should not be too hard on King Milinda. Even today one encounters questions that are just as foolish in connection with Buddhism and Buddhist beliefs. Particularly bad in this respect are the intellectuals of modern Japan, who in most cases have received a rather thorough education in European culture but know almost nothing about Indian thought or the wisdom of Buddhism. Thus with regard to Buddhism they are quite likely to display the same kind of ignorance and misunderstanding as was shown by King Milinda two thousand years ago.

It is meaningless to try to understand Japanese or East Asian culture, or even world culture for that matter, and at the same time ignore the influence of Buddhism. It is because so many Japanese have made no effort to understand Buddhism, which has been such a vital influence in the past, and have convinced themselves that if only they can master the spirit of Western rationalism they can completely comprehend world affairs, that we find ourselves faced with many of the problems we do today. By this I do not mean that we should immediately abandon Western rationalism and return to the wisdom of the East. It is not a question of choosing one or the other. What is important is to make a sincere and open-minded attempt to understand them both correctly.

This seems to have been what King Milinda did. He began his career as a military conqueror but later turned his energies to the task of understanding Indian thought through the medium of philosophical debate. Some time around the period between 160 and 140 B.C., he gained control of the Kabul region, in present day Afghanistan, and in the latter part of the second century B.C. invaded India, eventually extending his rule as far as central India. The Indians referred to him as "the greatest king in all India," and after his death his bones were distributed about the country and buried in many different places, as had been done earlier in the case of Shakyamuni. This last was probably done at his own request. Scholars surmise that he spoke some Indian language, and it is probable that he became rather thoroughly assimilated to the country and looked on it as his home.

If there is a sincere desire for mutual understanding, then barriers of race and nationality can always be transcended one way or another. King Milinda, who loved to converse and debate with others, found that for him that was the path to understanding.

The Wisdom of Nagasena

King Milinda, as we have seen, took every opportunity to meet with eminent monks and religious leaders and to engage them in debate. But for a long time he seemed unable to find anyone whom he could regard as a worthy opponent. It is related that he gave a great sigh and said: "All India is an empty thing, it is verily like chaff! There is no one, either recluse or Brahman, capable of discussing things with me, and dispelling my doubts."[3]

Such a state of affairs was certainly an embarrassment to Brahmans, Buddhists, and other religious groups of the time. In the introductory section of the *Questions of King Milinda*, we are told that the members of the Buddhist Order thereupon set about searching earnestly for a monk who would be capable of engaging with the king in debate.

It is at this point that Nagasena appears on the scene. We are told that having been born on the same day as a very large elephant, he was given the name Nagasena, *naga* being the word for elephant, an animal held in very high respect in India. The name Nagasena, it would appear, is intended to symbolize the fact that, just as

3. *Ibid*, p. 10.

Milinda is the head of the state, Nagasena is king in the world of thought.

According to the text, he was born into a Brahman family and at an early age showed a fondness for learning. He mastered the three *Vedas* while still a child, but later, declaring them to be "nonsense," left home, and became a Buddhist monk. Before long, this young monk had become known all over India for his unrivaled skill in discourse, and his reputation reached the ears of King Milinda in Shakala, the capital of his state.

It was inevitable that the two should meet in debate. But before that happened, we may suppose that Nagasena took every precaution possible to insure that he was prepared for the encounter, for he knew that the reputation of the entire Buddhist community depended upon his performance.

His opponent was a conqueror from another land. If he had been simply a political and military leader, Nagasena's task would not have been such a difficult one. The problem was that his opponent was also an intellectual of the highest order, steeped in the learning and culture of the West. Thus the encounter between these two men in effect represented a confrontation between the philosophy and wisdom of the East and that of the West. If Nagasena were bested in the debate, the result would be not only to destroy his own reputation, but perhaps to doom the entire Buddhist faith to a process of decline.

Nagasena undoubtedly had complete confidence in the greatness of the Dharma, though it must have required a good deal of courage and resolve to agree to the debate. When he reported his decision to his teacher Rohana, he is said to have remarked, "Not only let King Milinda, holy one, but let all the kings of India come and propound questions to me, and I will break all those puzzles up and solve them!"[4]

After Nagasena had entered the capital city of Shakala, the text gives the following description of him: "He was the leader of a company of the Order; the head of a body of disciples; the teacher of a school; famous and renowned, and highly esteemed by the people. And he was learned, clever, wise, sagacious, and able; a skilful expounder, of subdued manners, but full of courage; well versed in tradition, master of the three Baskets (Pitakas), and erudite

4. *Ibid*, p. 23.

in Vedic lore. He was in possession of the highest (Buddhist) insight, a master of all that had been handed down in the schools, and of the various discriminations by which the most abstruse points can be explained. He knew by heart the ninefold divisions of the doctrine of the Buddha to perfection, and was equally skilled in discerning both the spirit and the letter of the Word. Endowed with instantaneous and varied power of repartee, and wealth of language, and beauty of eloquence, he was difficult to equal, and still more difficult to excel, difficult to answer, to repel, or to refute. He was imperturbable as the depths of the sea, immovable as the king of mountains; victorious in the struggle with evil, a dispeller of darkness and diffuser of light; mighty in eloquence, a confounder of the followers of other masters, and a crusher-out of the adherents of rival doctrines."[5]

The text continues in this vein, in characteristic Indian fashion piling up the praises of Nagasena to the point of tedium. The passage was probably added by some later writer who wished to emphasize Nagasena's worthiness, though it is possible to read it as a generalized description of the kind of person who would serve as the ideal propagator of the Buddhist faith. However, since the text tells us that in the end Nagasena did in fact overcome the arguments of this famous king and representative of the Greek world and succeeded in converting him to Buddhism, perhaps the description is not so exaggerated after all.

If we examine the questions the king put to Nagasena and the answers he gave, we see that in fact he seems to have had great composure and agility of mind. Even those queries that almost any person would find himself hard pressed to answer he responds to with skillful analogies and cogent arguments in a way that is quite remarkable. Let us look, for example, at the famous passage which deals with the proof of the existence of the Buddha. It goes as follows:

" 'Have you, Nagasena, seen the Buddha?'
" 'No, Sire.'
" 'Then have your teachers seen the Buddha?'
" 'No, Sire.'
" 'Then, venerable Nagasena, there is no Buddha.' "[6]

5. *Ibid*, pp. 34–35.
6. *Ibid*, p. 109.

At this point we might ask ourselves how we would reply to this argument. Our opponent is a Greek and a positivist who wants proof based on empirical evidence. What evidence could we offer from Buddhist history that would give positive proof of the existence of Shakyamuni, we may be asking ourselves. But Nagasena proceeds in a different fashion.

" 'But, great king, have you seen the river Uha in the Himalaya mountains?'

" 'No, Sir.'

" 'Or has your father seen it?'

" 'No, Sir.'

" 'Then, your Majesty, is there therefore no such river?'

" 'It is there. Though neither I nor my father has seen it, it is nevertheless there.'

" 'Just so, great king, though neither I nor my teachers have seen the Blessed One, nevertheless there was such a person.'

" 'Very good, Nagasena!' "[7]

In this way, Nagasena convinced King Milinda of the existence of Shakyamuni. The dialogue is reminiscent of the kind of exchanges one finds in Zen writings or suggests a mere playing with words. And yet, depending upon how one looks at it, it can also be read as a profoundly suggestive and ironical criticism of the whole Western concept of existence. Nagasena's method of replying to the king's arguments is to present a series of questions of his own, which, as the king answers them, inevitably and in a natural fashion lead the king around to the point of agreeing with Nagasena's position. This, it seems to me, is an expression of true Oriental wisdom. In time, we are told, King Milinda came to admit that Nagasena was equal in wisdom to Shariputra, one of Shakyamuni's major disciples who was characterized as being "foremost in wisdom."

The analogy with the Uha River seems particularly apt. Many of the rivers of India have their sources far away among the Himalayas, swelling in size as they descend and bringing fertility to the land before they enter the sea. In the same manner, the teachings of Shakyamuni, originating far in the past, had by Nagasena's time spread throughout the country, enriching the minds and hearts of the Indian people. Shakyamuni had already been dead for several hundred years, but the fact that the religion he had founded had

7. *Ibid*, p. 109.

come to enjoy such a flourishing state was proof of his existence and greatness.

Western scholars in modern times have on occasion questioned whether Shakyamuni ever existed, and it is not surprising that men of earlier times, such as King Milinda, should have had similar doubts. But the king bases his argument upon the premise that only that which one can see with one's own eyes and touch with one's own hands truly exists, an assumption that, although it may be effective at times as a tool in determining the reliability of other people's views, is surely faulty in itself. There are many things that, although we cannot see or touch them, do in fact exist, and it is quite proper that we should believe in their existence. Nagasena, by showing up the narrowness of King Milinda's epistemology, demolishes it.

As has often been pointed out, there are certain types of thinking that seem to come naturally to Eastern peoples but which are difficult for Westerners to comprehend. That these two philosophers of the East and West, the monk Nagasena and the monarch Milinda, frankly and open-mindedly engaged in debate is of great significance. It is easy to understand why historians of both East and West attach such importance to the *Questions of King Milinda*.

The work is particularly valuable in revealing the particular doctrines of Buddhism that interested and sometimes perplexed the Greeks most, and shows how Buddhist believers went about explaining these doctrines to those not already familiar with them. In the following passage, for example, the king questions Nagasena concerning the concepts of karma, rebirth, and the absence of a permanent soul:

"The king said: 'What is it, Nagasena, that is reborn?'

" 'Name-and-form is reborn.'

" 'What, is it this same name-and-form that is reborn?'

" 'No; but by this name-and-form deeds are done, good or evil, and by these deeds (this Karma) another name-and-form is reborn.'

" 'If that be so, Sir, would not the new being be released from its evil Karma?'

"The Elder replied: 'Yes, if it were not reborn. But just because it is reborn, O king, it is therefore not released from its evil Karma.' "[8]

8. *Ibid*, pp. 72–73.

Here Nagasena is explaining that there is no permanent or eternal soul. The "name-and-form," that is, the mind and body, that make up a person in one existence are different from the mind and body the person has when reborn in another existence. He also points out that it is karma—the accumulation of good or evil actions in one existence—that provides the generative force for rebirth in another existence.

Buddhist philosophy teaches that sentient beings are made up of what are known as the *goon* or "five aggregates." Of these five, one, *shiki*, or "form," refers to the material or fleshly element in the being. The other four, perception, mental conceptions, volition, and consciousness of mind, all refer to the mental elements of the being. Since these five elements keep coming together to form a human being in successive existences, there is no permanent essence or soul in the human being.

We have seen that the karma or actions performed by a person in one existence are what cause the five aggregates to come together again and form a human being in a succeeding existence. The question, of course, is how the being of the former existence is related to the being of the later existence. Examining the answers Nagasena has given in the passage quoted above, we would have to conclude that the two beings are neither identical nor non-identical. As has often been pointed out, Indian thought frequently makes use of such concepts, which are made up of seemingly opposite and contradictory terms. We must understand this concept of identity that is simultaneously non-identity if we are to understand the Buddhist view of rebirth or transmigration, with its denial of the existence of a permanent soul. We of course must also understand the concept of karma, which provides the motivating force in this process.

When properly understood, these Buddhist doctrines of transmigration make very good sense even today. By contrast, the doctrine that there is an eternal soul or essence which continues in existence while passing through the process of transmigration seems to be rather too rigid and to present a number of contradictions.

Nagasena goes on to give the king various ingenious illustrations in order to make clear to him the way in which a being of a former existence is related to one of a later existence through the force of karma. In the end, he succeeds in convincing the king of the truth of the doctrine. Such passages demonstrate how Buddhism was able to support its doctrines with eloquent and logically convincing arguments similar to those employed in Greek philosophy.

After King Milinda and Nagasena had completed two very lengthy and profound discussions of Buddhist philosophy, we find the following descriptive passage:

"Then the king, pleased with the explanations given of the questions he had put, had Nagasena robed in an embroidered cloak worth a hundred thousand, and said to him: 'Venerable Nagasena, I hereby order that you shall be provided with your daily meal for eight hundred days; and give you the choice of anything in the palace that it is lawful for you to take.' And when the Elder refused, saying he had enough to live on, the king rejoined: 'I know, Sir, you have enough to live on. But you should both protect me and protect yourself — yourself from the possibility of a public rumor to the effect that you convinced me but received nothing from me, and me from the possibility of a public rumor that though I was convinced, I would give nothing in acknowledgement.'

" 'Let it be as you wish, great king,' was the reply."[9]

After the two had parted and Nagasena had returned to his hermitage, each of the two men thought over the course of their discussions and found themselves pleased with the results. Both came to the conclusion that the king had asked good questions and the sage had answered them suitably. It should be noted that the king did not feel pleased with himself because of the clever or incisive way in which he questioned Nagasena, nor did Nagasena congratulate himself on the keenness and eloquence with which he had answered the most difficult inquiries. The source of both men's satisfaction lay in their having been able to put aside personal feelings and prejudices and to engage in an earnest search for the truth. This tells us much about the meaning of human sincerity and the nature of true dialogue.

The Debate of Wise Men and of Kings

Before beginning his historic debates with King Milinda, Nagasena first attempted to determine the grounds upon which they

9. *Ibid*, pp. 134-5.

would be held, as recorded in the following famous passage:

"The king said, 'Reverand Sir, will you discuss with me?'

" 'If your Majesty will discuss as a scholar, well; but if you will discuss as a king, no.'

" 'How is it then that scholars discuss?'

" 'When scholars talk a matter over one with another, then is there a winding up, an unravelling; one or the other is convicted of error, and he then acknowledges his mistake; distinctions are drawn, and contra-distinctions; and yet thereby they are not angered. Thus do scholars, O king, discuss.'

" 'And how do kings discuss?'

" 'When a king, your Majesty, discusses a matter, and he advances a point, if any one differ from him on that point, he is apt to fine him, saying, 'Inflict such and such a punishment upon that fellow!' Thus, your Majesty, do kings discuss.'

" 'Very well. It is as a scholar, not as a king, that I will discuss. Let your reverence talk unrestrainedly, as you would with a brother, or a novice, or a lay disciple, or even with a servant. Be not afraid!'

" 'Very good, your Majesty,' said Nagasena, with thankfulness."[10]

Nagasena wishes to insure at the outset that philosophical positions and political authority will be clearly distinguished. Men who wield political power have a well-known tendency to try to impose their opinions upon others through the weight of their authority, and if this fails, to resort to force to bring their opponent to submission. But this procedure will never lead to the discovery of truth and cannot be called a true philosophical debate or a debate of wise men. Indeed, it is not even an appropriate procedure for kings, since an assent forced from others does not come from the heart and is worthless.

Buddhist scholars have often referred to this passage as an early example of the concept of freedom of speech and inquiry. People in general tend to think of freedom of speech as an ideal of democracy that only came to be clearly recognized in Europe in recent centuries. But as we see, in ancient India there was already a forum for the free exchange of ideas. In part this is no doubt due to the temperament of the Indian people, with their devotion to the ideal of *dharma* or righteousness, but the concept was further strengthened by the spread of Buddhist thought.

10. *Ibid*, p. 46.

The text records a total of 262 questions debated by King Milinda and Nagasena. It is said that there were also a number of questions the discussion of which was not recorded, the complete total being 304.

Nagasena replies to each of the king's questions in a clear, striking, and wholly appropriate manner, and at the conclusion of each section pertaining to a particular question, the king says, "You are right. Nagasena, I realize that it is just as you have said." In this way the reader is led step by step through the various aspects of Buddhist belief until, before he realizes it, he has mastered its most profound and fundamental truths.

The book thus serves as an introduction to Buddhism, and for this reason was later used in Theravada Buddhism as a manual of instruction for the monks. Indeed, it was probably with some such purpose in mind that the compiler or compilers put together this record of the debate.

Among the many questions treated, the text has a very interesting passage on the meaning of the term *shakubuku*, which designates one of the two attitudes to be adopted in preaching and bringing salvation to others. Reading this, one can see that King Milinda's understanding of the term contained errors and misconceptions very similar to those held by many people today regarding the Soka Gakkai's use of the term.

"The king first quotes a saying of the Buddha, 'Punish him who deserves punishment,' and then goes on to say: 'Now punishment [*shakubuku*], Nagasena, means the cutting off of hands or feet, flogging, casting into bonds, torture, execution, degradation in rank. Such a saying is therefore not worthy of the Blessed One, and he ought not to have made use of it.' "[11]

One is at a loss how even to describe such misunderstanding. Though the term probably had slightly different connotations two thousand years ago from what it has in present day usage, the misconception that *shakubuku* means "violence," and the criticisms and slanders that result from such a misconception, are the same, past and present.

"Nagasena proceeds to reply to King Milinda's objection by explaining that the term which stands for *shakubuku* here does not mean to punish but rather to subdue, and is used in contrast to the

11. *Ibid*, p. 254.

term *shōju*, meaning to cultivate. He goes on to remark: 'The proud heart, great king, is to be subdued, and the lowly heart cultivated — the wicked heart to be subdued, and the good heart to be cultivated — carelessness of thought is to be subdued, and exactness of thought to be cultivated — he who is given over to wrong views is to be subdued, and he who has attained to right views is to be cultivated — he who is not noble is to be subdued, and the noble one is to be cultivated — the robber is to be subdued, and the honest brother is to be cultivated.' "[12]

King Milinda then came to realize that he had been mistaken in his understanding and in the end acknowledged the correctness of Nagasena's explanation. He had, in effect, been subjected to the process of *shakubuku* by Nagasena.

According to the text, the king in the end was filled with great joy, all of his doubts concerning the Three Treasures of the Buddha, the Dharma, and the Sangha having been resolved. Casting aside his personal pride and arrogance, he attained great purity of faith. He became a lay believer of the Buddhist Order and donated a monastery named Milinda to it. Furthermore, it is said that later in life he relinquished the throne to his son and became a monk, in time gaining the status of an arhat.

This was a period of transition when Mahayana Buddhism, with its emphasis upon the importance of the lay believer, was about to sweep to the fore in India, and perhaps because of its influence, the spirit of *shakubuku*, the active and aggressive attitude that seeks to make new converts to the faith, is reflected throughout the text we have been discussing. Certainly the spirit of Nagasena, who through *shakubuku* succeeded in converting a monarch, is directly allied to the spirit of the later followers of Mahayana Buddhism. And the debate between these two philosophers of East and West represented a kind of public confrontation of beliefs. Thus we can see that by the second century B.C. Buddhism had already begun to exercise an important influence upon the Greek world of the West.

In the section that follows, I would like to examine the nature of that influence in greater detail, as well as to discuss the spread of Buddhism southward to Sri Lanka and Burma and eastward into China.

12. *Ibid*, pp. 255–6.

5

Cultural Exchange between East and West

The Turning Point in East-West Relations

It was during the reign of King Ashoka that Buddhism first began to spread beyond the borders of India and to exert an influence upon other cultural spheres. But the process did not get into full swing until around the beginning of the Christian era, or some five hundred years after the death of the Buddha. (Of course, as I have explained in my earlier volume, we have no way to determine the exact date of the Buddha's death, and so we can only speak in general figures.)

It is interesting in this connection to note the theory of the three periods after the death of the Buddha. According to this theory, which was propounded mainly by the Mahayana Buddhists, the death of the Buddha was destined to be followed by a period known as the *Shōbō* or Correct Law, a second period known as *Zōhō* or Imitation Law, and a third known as *Mappō* or End of the Law. As the names indicate, the theory was based upon the view that the understanding and practice of the Dharma would gradually decline over the centuries until the doctrine disappeared altogether. There are different assertions as to just how long the first two periods will last, but one of the most common is that the first period would be of five hundred years' duration. In other words, five hundred years after Shakyamuni's decease, the correct understanding of his teachings would begin to decline.

Scholarly research seems to indicate that the original form of the theory viewed the period of the Correct Law as being fifty years in duration. During this time, the *Shōmon*, the disciples who had received instruction directly from the Buddha himself, would one by one have departed from the world, Buddhism would enter an entirely new era, and the Order would face its first major crisis. The assumption is that Shakyamuni propounded this view to his followers not as a prophesy of future events but as a warning to them: after his death they should take particular care to see that his teachings were handed down correctly to later ages.

The Buddhist Order apparently passed through the first predicted period of crisis without great difficulty, and it then gradually came to be believed that the period of the Correct Law would last not fifty but five hundred years. The *Questions of King Milinda* seems to have been put into its present form sometime around the beginning of the Christian era, and it contains the following passage concerning the period of the Correct Law. The disciple Ananda has persuaded Shakyamuni to allow women to enter the Buddhist Order, though the latter clearly has misgivings about the wisdom of the move. Shakyamuni then says, "The good law [Correct Law], Ananda, would endure for a thousand years if no women had been admitted to the Order. But now, Ananda, it will only last five hundred years."[1]

Any woman today will probably be enraged by such a prejudiced attitude, even if she does not happen to be a supporter of so-called women's liberation. But in Shakyamuni's time this was apparently the commonly accepted view of women and their deleterious influence.

The theory that the period of the Correct Law would last for five hundred years seems to have been reinforced by the sense of danger and crisis actually prevailing in the Buddhist Order at this time. The religious organization, which believed itself to be duty bound to hand down the teachings of Shakyamuni in their correct form, had in fact split up into a number of mutually exclusive groups. The study of the *Abhidharma* or exegetical works of the canon had become increasingly complex and time consuming, and the monks grew more and more isolated from the populace as a whole. It was precisely because of this state of affairs that the Mahayana movement, with its emphasis upon the importance of the lay believer, rose to widespread prominence around five hundred years after the death of the Buddha.

I shall discuss in greater detail later the factors that led to the rise

1. *Ibid*, p. 186.

of the Mahayana movement. But before leaving the subject of the three periods, I may note that the version of the theory prevalent in Japan led the Japanese of the late Heian period, the eleventh and twelfth centuries, to believe that they were entering the period of *Mappō*. This view was no doubt reinforced by the troubled social conditions of the time, and it in turn profoundly affected the attitude toward religion and life. In China as well, the view that the world was entering upon the period of the End of the Law came to the fore at times when the country was in a stage of social disorder and decline.

I would like now to examine the cultural relations between India and her neighbors in this period five hundred years after the death of the Buddha. We have seen that, in the reign of King Ashoka in the third century B.C., envoys were sent to convey a knowledge of Buddhism to the states to the west, and from this period on, India seems to have maintained a relatively active process of cultural exchange with these states. In order to understand the steps by which Buddhism was able to develop into a major world religion, it is highly important that we pay close attention to these cultural exchanges between East and West.

The *Questions of King Milinda* provides us with one example of how Buddhist thought exerted an influence upon the Greek world. But we must not overlook the fact that the process also worked the other way around, the West at times exerting a strong influence over the Indian world. Alexander the Great, it will be recalled, invaded India in the fourth century B.C., and the influences set in motion by that event had by the time we are dicussing become apparent in many different aspects of Indian life. Alexander himself stayed in India for no longer than a few months, but he left garrisons there and in the areas to the west, and Greek rulers of one kind or another continued off and on for the following two hundred years to control parts of India. And after the fall of the Greek kingdoms, the Scyths, who were strongly influenced by Hellenic culture, continued in their place to rule parts of India for several centuries more. As a result of these Greek and Scythian invasions, Buddhism was brought into cultural contact with the Hellenic world. One of the results is the famous Buddhist statuary of the Gandharan school, which flourished in northwest India under the patronage of the Scyths.

It is interesting to note that in the Buddhist art of the centuries preceding this strong Hellenic influence, Shakyamuni himself is never depicted. Thus, for example, in a sculptural relief portraying the Buddha's attainment of enlightenment, only the Bodhi tree under which he meditated and the mat he sat on when he attained enlightenment are shown, these two objects serving to symbolize the presence of Shakyamuni. But in the art of Gandhara, Shakyamuni is portrayed in sculpture in the same manner as were the gods of Greece and Rome. This would appear to be an example of Western ways of thought exercising an influence upon the Indian mind. It is also said that some aspects of Mahayana Buddhist doctrine were derived from Western thought, but we shall leave the discussion of that question for a later chapter.

Just at the time we are discussing, another great world religion, Christianity, was making its appearance in Palestine. For both the Eastern world centered about India and the Western world centered about the Roman Empire, it seems to have been a period of turmoil and transition. In India, the Greek kings were replaced by other foreign invaders, and both Brahmanism and Buddhism had lost their vitality and hardened into a rigid formalism. To the west, the Roman Republic gave way to the Roman Empire, which extended its power over the entire Mediterranean world and beyond and weighed ever more heavily upon the people under its rule, particularly those in the conquered lands along the border.

In this period of change and unrest, people looked hopefully for the appearance of a hero, or searched about them for a savior of souls. In India men awaited the appearance of the bodhisattva Maitreya, whom Shakyamuni had predicted would come into the world in some future time to bring salvation, while the Jews looked longingly for their Messiah. One cannot help but be struck by the similarities in East and West, which this attitude of unease and anticipation reflects.

It was a time of spiritual darkness and despair. But it is precisely at such times, when the darkness is deepest and when human civilization seems to be facing certain doom, that men long most fervently for the appearance of a great new philosophy or religion. And, as though in response to this, a great thinker or religious leader actually does appear to light the way for mankind.

In Palestine a new religion, founded upon the doctrines of Judaism but addressed to all peoples everywhere, was coming into being. In India, the Mahayana movement was similarly making its

71

appearance. If Buddhism had remained at the stage of development represented by the Hinayana school of the time, it would probably never have become a major world religion. But through the impetus of the Mahayana movement, it became an actively proselytizing religion, spreading eastward to China and Japan, and to the lands to the west as well.

Buddhism and Christianity

Most comparative studies of Buddhism and Christianity in the past have tended to focus upon the differences between the two religions, as Fumio Masutani's does. The cultural and intellectual climate of East and West naturally differed to some extent, and it is only natural that the religions that emerged from the two regions should differ.

It is extremely interesting to note, however, that recently this tendency has begun to change and scholars are starting to emphasize the points that the two religions have in common. Perhaps the time has passed when we can go on thinking in terms of this hard and fast dualism of East and West. What is wanted in our present age is a consciousness of world unity and oneness. Thus, although we may continue to some extent to discuss the ways in which East and West differ, it is far more important to look for basic similarities and points of agreement. I need hardly add that at a time like this to go beyond the discussion of differences and attempt to establish the superiority of one of the religions over the other would be sheer nonsense.

India, we must not forget, has from early times been a meeting ground for the cultures of East and West, and racially as well it represents a mixture of peoples from both regions. Thus the Indians have probably never had as sharp a consciousness of their "Easternness" as we Japanese customarily have.

The cultural anthropologist Tadao Umesao argues that the region of western Asia from India to the Mediterranean should be regarded as a "Central Region" distinct from both East and West. As we have seen in our discussion of the *Questions of King Milinda*, this region of western Asia was from early times the scene of constant cultural exchange, and should perhaps indeed be viewed as a single Central Region. If we adopt the approach advocated by Umesao, then both Buddhism and Christianity become products of the same world.

Whether we accept this viewpoint or not, there is no denying that Christianity and Buddhism are alike in preaching to all mankind a universal message on how one ought to live. The origins of most religions are to be found in matters pertaining to sacrifice and the invocation of supernatural powers, and such religions customarily exhibit a very close connection with organs of political control in a tribal society. But no such political element is to be found in the genesis of either Christianity or Buddhism. On the contrary, both seem to have been born in a climate of opposition to political power. And for this reason, their respective histories are often characterized by persecution at the hands of the men in power.

These two great religions, we may say, exist on a higher plane than those that are narrowly bound to the performance of sacrificial duties for some particular political body, aiming rather at the creation of values for humankind as a whole. This is what both Shakyamuni and Jesus sought to do in their teachings, and their followers, whose duty it was to put such teachings into practice, inevitably, because of the nature of the teachings, thought in terms of a universal appeal and set out to bring salvation to all mankind.

Some Buddhist scholars have speculated that the concept of salvation in Christianity actually derives from the ideal of the bodhisattva, the potential Buddha who postpones his own salvation in order to assist others, which evolved in Mahayana Buddhism. It has also been suggested that Jesus may have had some connection with the Essenes, a Judaic sect numbering some four thousand members who, in the century before Christ, lived on the shore of the Dead Sea in monastic groups very similar to those of the Buddhist Order. Originally, of course, since Judaism was the religion of the Jewish state and society, there was within it no concept of the monk who withdraws from society in order to live a life of austerity and religious practices. The fact that the Essenes did just this suggests that, though customarily described as a sect of Judaism, they were influenced by the Buddhist concept of the Sangha or monastic order.

Professor Hajime Nakamura offers a number of other examples of possible or probable Buddhist influence in the West. According to him, remains of Buddhist monasteries have been found in northern Europe, and in 1954 a small Buddhist statue was discovered in Sweden. It has even been suggested that Buddhism had spread to the British Isles before the introduction of Christianity. This thesis rests upon a statement made by Origen in his commentary on the Book of Ezekiel, written around 230, which says: "In that island [Britain], the Druid priests and Buddhists have already spread teachings concerning the oneness of God, and for that reason the inhabitants already are inclined toward it [Christianity]." We can only be amazed that Buddhist influence should have spread even to the Celts in the British Isles at the very western edge of Europe.

Although some of the monks and envoys who were responsible for spreading the Buddhist teachings over so vast an area may have traveled by ship or on horseback, there is no doubt that most of them went on foot. Reading the lives of Shakyamuni and Jesus, one is impressed by how much walking they did. And the disciples who spread their teachings must have done much more. The Buddhist monks, fired with a determination to bring salvation to all men, spread out in all directions from the Indian subcontinent, pushing on through the most forbidding terrain. With such ardor to sustain them, it is not surprising that they should have carried the teachings of Buddhism even as far as the British Isles.

Excavations at the site of an ancient town in southern Wales have reportedly turned up a large number of Roman coins, and among them is one coin from the kingdom of King Milinda. As we have seen, King Milinda or Menander ruled a part of northwestern India in the second century B.C. It would be fascinating if we could somehow trace the coin's journey as it passed from India to the Roman Empire and thence to its western outpost in Britain.

While the coin was still in India, it may well have witnessed the rise of the Mahayana movement. Then, passing from the hand of some wealthy merchant, the kind who, as a lay believer, did so much to lend financial support to the Mahayana monks, it began its journey west. Along the way, it may have heard rumors of the tragic death of a savior in the region of Palestine. Eventually it found its way into the hands of a Roman merchant or soldier who collected rare coins, and thus became one of the group of coins found in Wales.

In any event, it would be a fact of great significance if Buddhism had indeed reached as far as Britain in this early period. England has been very active in Buddhist studies in modern times, and though this derives in part from India, with its Buddhist sites and relics, having once been under British rule, I cannot help wondering if it does not result from some uncanny connection from the past.

A number of European philosophers in recent centuries have also taken a great interest in Indian Buddhism. In the afterword to a work by Kenshi Hori, the author quotes the following words of the great German philosopher Schopenhauer: "Some day a Biblical scholar who is also thoroughly versed in Indian religion will, on the basis of careful and detailed evidence, succeed in making clear the connections between Christianity and the religions of India." These words made a deep impression on Professor Hori when he was a young man, and he proceeded to devote the following thirty years to precisely the problem of clarifying this relationship.

The results of his research have recently appeared in a work entitled *Bukkyō to Kirisutokyō*. In this, he mentions that in 1958 a French archeological expedition working in Afghanistan discovered an edict inscription of King Ashoka written in both Greek and Aramaic. The discovery caused considerable excitement in academic circles and attracted Professor Hori's attention in particular because of the use of Aramaic. Aramaic was the common language throughout the Persian Empire, which at the height of its power extended from the Indus Valley in the east through southwest Asia and as far as Nubia in Egypt. It was accordingly the everyday language of Palestine in the time of Jesus. It is possible to speculate that Jesus could have gained a knowledge of Buddhism through such writings in Aramaic and could have been influenced by its teachings.

We tend naturally to think of this whole region of western and central Asia and India in terms of the way it exists today. But conditions were quite different there in the centuries just before and after the Christian era. Central Asia in particular was at that time a veritable crossroads for commerce and cultural exchange between east and west, north and south. Cities along the caravan routes served as centers for the dissemination of ideas and material culture, and the famous Silk Road linking Ch'ang-an in China with Rome in the west passed through the area. The Mongol conquest led by Genghis Khan devastated the region and left it the virtual wilderness that it is today, but excavations have demonstated how flourishing its condition was in ancient times.

The whole area from Persia to central Asia in the period we are discussing constituted a single great cultural sphere, communicating with those of China to the east, India to the south, and Rome to the west, and in effect was perhaps more advanced and cosmopolitan than any of these others. There is nothing remarkable, therefore, in supposing that persons in Palestine, on the western edge of this cultural sphere, had received some news of the Mahayana movement, which had arisen in northwest India on the eastern edge of the sphere. The remarkable thing would be to suppose that they had not.

The Conditions for a World Religion

In his studies, Professor Hajime Nakamura has not only discussed the influence of Buddhism on Christianity but has touched upon the question of Buddhist influence on Greek philosophy as well. Since Greece is generally regarded as the birthplace of Western philosophy, we should naturally expect, in view of what has been said above about cultural exchanges between the two worlds, that Western philosophy should have been subjected in some degree to Buddhist influence, albeit indirectly. We may note to begin with that both Buddhism and Greek philosophy share a common concern with such problems as the true nature of life, of existence, and of the individual.

The Socratic injunction "Know thyself" is justly famous, but Shakyamuni also said, "You would do well to examine and reflect upon yourselves." In the Buddhist scriptures there is no end to the passages that call for such self-reflection. "So I say to you, Ananda. You should use yourself as a lamp, use yourself as a point of reliance, and not rely on others. You should use the Dharma as a lamp, use the Dharma as a point of reliance, and not rely on other things." Again, "The point of reliance for the self is none other than the self. What other point of reliance should there be? When the self has been controlled and regulated, then one has gained a point of reliance that is difficult to acquire."

Broadly speaking, both religion and philosophy arise out of man's reflections upon the nature of the world and of human existence, and upon his consciousness of his identity as a human being. The concept of Original Sin in Christianity and the Buddhist way of life that seeks to free one from the evils of human desire are both expressions of man's intense spirit of striving for salvation. They are intimately tied up with human ideals and the search for a universally valid way of life.

The statement may seem an extreme one, but I do not believe that any amount of change in social systems or organizations will bring improvement in the world unless man himself, the creator and controller of such systems and organizations, is somehow changed. Religion and philosophy, rather than aiming at a reform of social institutions, hold that it is essential first to bring about a reform in the inner nature of the individual. That is, they take the view that without a human revolution there can be no social revolution.

Glancing over the record of revolutionary activities in world history, we will note that the revolutions carried out on the basis of some preceding revolution in the consciousness of the people as a whole have been the ones that were most thoroughgoing in scope and most lasting in effect. By contrast, those imposed upon the population by force and the use of arms have entailed great sacrifice and suffering and yet have been relatively short-lived in effect. In this respect we should take special notice of both Buddhism and Christianity, which have continued for two thousand years or more to serve as a support to countless numbers of peoples of East and West and have defined for them the ideals by which they should live.

Lafcadio Hearn in his *Literary Criticism East and West* states the opinion that most of the legends and fables of the Old World could be traced back to Buddhist origins. As a matter of fact, studies in comparative folklore have shown that a number of Western fairy tales do indeed derive from Buddhist and Indian sources. Moreover, the famous Biblical parable of the prodigal son, as has often been pointed out, has an almost exact parallel in the Lotus Sutra. Such parallels once again suggest that there must have been some connection between Buddhism and Christianity.

Even if there were no direct contacts, I think we are safe in making the following assertion. Whenever men set out in earnest to discover the true nature of human life, even though there may be differences in their methods or angle of approach, they are bound to reach a certain number of common conclusions. The development of both Buddhism and Christianity to the stature of world religions indicates to me that they are in possession of certain universal truths. Because of the way in which they apprehend the nature of man and delve into the essence of the phenomenal world, they are capable of convincing millions of people of the validity of their teachings, and it is this capability that has allowed them to become world religions.

Western philosophy, and Christianity in particular, has over long periods of time occupied itself with the investigation of such difficult concepts as immortality and the proof of the existence of God. In a similar manner, such Buddhist concepts as transmigration, karma, and dependent origination have led to a wealth of philosophical speculation. If these two religions had never come into being to challenge men to philosophical debate and speculation, the intellectual history of mankind would undoubtedly be much shallower.

Professor Nakamura has singled out three factors which he believes enabled Buddhism and Christianity to develop to the stature of universal religions. First, they made a conscious attempt to combat the incantatory elements and other magical beliefs and practices of the more primitive religions. Second, they rejected the systems of sacrifice supported by the established religions. Even their methods of denial were similar, the Buddhists comparing the Brahmans to blind men, the Christians using the same comparison in their denunciation of the Pharisees. Third, they both succeeded in transcending the narrow concepts of race, class, and nationality. In Buddhism this took the form of an insistence upon the equality of the four traditional classes of Indian society, while in Christianity it meant a rejection of the distinction between Jew and Gentile.

We have touched on the first two of these factors in the discussion above. The third, the ability to rise above distinctions of race and nationality, is of course a necessary condition if the religion is to spread beyond the region of its origin. This condition, which allowed Buddhism to travel east to China and southeast Asia and west to the Hellenic world, was already present as a fundamental tenet as early as two thousand years ago, as demonstrated in the following passage from the *Questions of King Milinda*: "For if grounded in virtue, and careful in attention — whether in the land of the Scythians or the Greeks, whether in China or Tartary, whether in Alexandria or in Nikumba, whether in Benares or in Kosala, whether in Kashmire or in Gandhara, whether on a mountain top or in the highest heavens — wheresoever he may be, the man who orders his life aright will realise Nirvana."[2]

2. *Ibid*, Part II, Vol. XXXVI, pp. 203-4.

In contrast to Brahmanism, which rested firmly upon the rigid four-class division of Indian society, Buddhism from the first showed itself superior to distinctions of class and nationality and was therefore able to develop into a world religion. Moreover, it did not seek a merely formal rejection of the divisions of class, race, or nationality. It would be more accurate to say that, since the ultimate aim of the religion and the core of its doctrine lie in the preaching of the equality and dignity of all men and the application of that principle in practice, it had of necessity to transcend all such distinctions both in form and in spirit.

As history has shown, the light born from the profound insights of the Buddha has proved capable of shining far beyond the borders of any particular national or racial group, and of illuminating the lives of men throughout the world and filling them with hope. This has come about not simply because the message of Buddhism has been transmitted by men and women from one nation or racial group to another, but rather because Buddhism possesses universal truths transcending national differences and capable of inspiring in people everywhere the conviction that the religion was especially created with their own needs and longings in mind.

It is this loftiness of wisdom, this doctrinal breadth and depth, and this invariable rejection of class distinctions and narrow racial and national concepts that qualify Buddhism and Christianity to be termed world religions. And in attempting to decide what power and effectiveness these religions may have to change the state of present day society, it is these essential qualities, rather than any superficial considerations of religious practice or dogma, that must be kept in mind.

6

The Rise of Mahayana Buddhism

Origins of the Mahayana Movement

I have referred on several previous occasions to the rise of the Mahayana movement, which took place somewhere around five hundred years after the death of the Buddha. Because of the dearth of reliable sources that would give any clear or concrete picture of just how and why the movement came about, the subject is fraught with speculation. I would like here to sort out and review the various theories that have been put forward concerning its origin and try to determine what significance the appearance of Mahayana Buddhism has in the history of Buddhism as a whole.

The subject is one of great importance since, in my opinion at least, if the Mahayana movement had not occurred, it is unlikely that Buddhism would ever have spread east to China, Korea, and Japan. The Theravada school of Buddhism was, as we have seen, essentially a monastic order whose members deliberately removed themselves from ordinary society so that they could practice their rigorous discipline. This type of religious organization is by its very nature lacking in the proselytizing spirit and is difficult for the ordinary members of society to participate in.

Moreover, the Chinese and Japanese, in contrast to the Indians, tend to be of a practical and down-to-earth mind, and it is unlikely that Hinayana thought, with its dry psychological and metaphysical treatises, would have had a very great appeal to them. Even if it had been introduced to these countries, it would probably have been of interest only to a small proportion of the population and would almost certainly have died out long ago. We customarily speak of China, Korea, and Japan as countries that were "destined for

Mahayana." This may seem a too deterministic way to state the matter, and yet it would in fact appear that it was only because Mahayana rather than Hinayana Buddhism was introduced to them that they in time became Buddhist.

In India as well, although we have seen how Buddhism flourished under the reign of King Ashoka in the third century B.C., Brahmanism from that time on began to regain power and Buddhism followed a path of steady decline. This occurred because, while Brahmanism was thoroughly integrated into Indian society as a whole, Buddhism showed an increasing tendency to withdraw and isolate itself from the general populace. At the same time it was beset by a spirit of sectarianism that precipitated repeated rifts in the religious organization, thus further isolating the various schools or sects of Buddhism from one another.

Glancing at the history of this period, we see that the Mauryan dynasty, of which Ashoka had been the outstanding ruler, came to an end around 180 B.C. It was replaced in western India by the Shunga dynasty, which was founded by a Brahman military leader and supported Brahmanism as the official doctrine of the state. Shortly after, around the middle of the first century B.C., a conqueror named King Kharavela appeared in the region of Kalinga in southeast India who was an enthusiastic follower of the Jain religion. As a result of these events, Buddhism was for a considerable period of time deprived of much of its support or subjected to outright persecution. During this period, sad to say, the trend toward disunity continued, and it broke apart into eighteen or twenty different sects, which wrangled continuously with one another.

In any organization, there is nothing more to be feared than the sowers of internal dissension, those who would bring about disruption within the group. This is particularly true of groups founded upon certain ideological or philosophical principles, for internal factionalism and contention usually spell destruction for the principles upheld by the group. This occurs because the members of the organization become so engrossed in the struggle to maintain dominance and combat rival factions that ideological principles are forgotten and, as a result, cease to function effectively even within the group, much less receive proper dissemination outside it. It is particularly deplorable to see Buddhism fall victim to sectarianism resulting from the egoism of its practitioners, since one of its basic aims is to shed light upon the inner nature of man and help him learn to overcome the demon of egoism that lies within him.

The Mahayana movement that sprang up in many regions of India at this time may in one sense be seen as an attempt to reform the religion and to combat the factionalism and strife that had come to characterize the Buddhist Order in its traditional form. It was a Buddhist equivalent of the Reformation in Europe, a movement to restore vitality to the faith. That the Buddhist Order faced the danger of political antagonism or outright persecution only served to strengthen in the leaders of the Mahayana movement their consciousness of themselves as Buddhists and their determination to fight for their beliefs.

How to cope with political pressure was one of the most important questions facing the Buddhists at this time. And here I believe we may distinguish a subtle difference in the ways in which the Hinayana and the Mahayana schools responded to such pressure.

The Mahayana Buddhists, as we have seen, chose to refer to the Theravada school as the Hinayana or Lesser Vehicle, a term surely intended as a mark of opprobrium. One reason for their disapproval, I believe, was that the Theravada tended to remain aloof from politics. Stated bluntly, we might say that its followers fled from reality and elected to take refuge in the seclusion of monastic life. For this reason their political position was characteristically vague and their attitude toward Brahmanism, which by now had become the state religion, more or less conciliatory.

Buddhists of the Mahayana school, on the other hand, disputed with the Brahmans and worked actively to oppose them. They conceived of Buddhism as a faith to be vigorously disseminated throughout society as a whole, not merely practiced by monks confined in a cloister. Various sutras and treatises of the Mahayana school describe the ideal king and the ways in which he should exercise power, and they do not hesitate to make political pronouncements on the basis of the ideals of Buddhism as embodied in the Dharma. The political pressures brought to bear upon them were consequently all the greater, yet at the same time they demonstrated by their attitude that they possessed the energy and determination to combat these pressures and to challenge the existing social order. Herein, I would say, lies one of the differences that distinguished the Mahayana from the Hinayana school.

Though dissatisfaction with the apolitical attitude of the Hinayanaists was among the factors leading to the rise of the Mahayana school, the problem of the proper relationship between politics and religion is a highly complex one and cannot be settled in haste. No doubt the Theravadins and other sects of traditional Buddhism had their own reasons for remaining aloof from political concerns. They looked upon the preservation of the orthodox teachings of Buddhism and the transmission of these teachings to posterity as their most important function. They probably feared that if they took a stand in political matters, they would invite interference and repression to an extent that would endanger the realization of their aim.

We must remember that Shakyamuni himself was born a member of the Kshatriya or ruling class, the eldest son of the king of the Shakya state and the logical successor to the throne. Nevertheless, he chose to relinquish his birthright and go out into the world as a wandering mendicant in order to seek a higher goal. He deliberately turned away from a political career so that he might learn to become a leader in the realm of the spirit and master the universal truths of human life. This was the stance he took, this was the task he set himself, one which concerned the eternal future of all mankind.

Lest I be misunderstood, let me clarify one point here. Although I believe politics and religion exist on essentially quite different levels, I am not saying that for that reason it is proper or even permissible for a man of religion to hold himself aloof from social and political concerns. After Shakyamuni attained enlightenment under the Bodhi tree, he did not remain alone, gloating over his newfound truths. Instead he set out upon a journey to preach and spread the Dharma so that he might share his enlightenment and wisdom with all men and women everywhere.

The tendency among the Theravadins and other early sects of Buddhism was quite different from this. The monks of these sects, virtually removed from all secular power and authority, increasingly shut themselves up in the hills and forests, devoting all their attention to the study of the treatises of the *Abhidharma*. By doing this, they appear to have sought only their own spiritual advancement and to have taken no steps to assist the advancement of others by preaching and offering guidance.

Here again the followers of the Mahayana movement differed from the older sects, insisting that it was necessary not only to work at one's own religious practice and salvation but at the same time to disseminate the teachings as widely as possible among the masses who were sunk in misery and delusion. This, they asserted, was to act in the true spirit of Shakyamuni. The goal of the Hinayana Buddhist was to achieve the status of an arhat or saint, while that of the Mahayana Buddhist was to achieve the status of bodhisattva, the enlightened being who vows to help others to salvation.

Reading the Mahayana scriptures, one is invariably struck with the degree to which they are designed to challenge society. We will have occasion to examine this point more fully when we come to discuss the Vimalakirti Sutra, which centers about the famous lay believer Vimalakirti and describes the very active role he played in the society of his time. Because of this fact, scholars have been led to suggest that, while Hinayana Buddhism was centered about the monastic community, Mahayana Buddhism was a movement that arose among the lay believers of the period.

This seems to me plausible enough, but I do not think we should regard Mahayana Buddhism as by any means a movement of the laity alone. We must remember that in India at the time we are discussing it was customary to hold monks in very high esteem, and it is unlikely that the laity would have proceeded entirely on their own without some sanction or support from members of the monastic community. Moreover, Mahayana displays a loftiness and complexity in doctrine that suggest the influence of the professional theologian and philosopher. My own guess would be that certain unusually keen and enlightened members of the monastic community, dissatisfied with the attitude and practices of Hinayana Buddhism, joined forces with the more spirited and imaginative leaders among the laity in a cooperative venture to carry out reforms.

In the famous poet-monk Ashvaghosha and the philosopher Nagarjuna, we can see examples of outstanding monks who began as followers of the Hinayana and later shifted to the Mahayana. Ashvaghosha, who lived and wrote in the first or second century A.D., received his original ordination and training in the Sarvastivada school, one of the important branches of the Hinayana, but eventually became a Mahayana follower. Similarly, Nagarjuna, who lived in the second or third century A.D., and the fifth century philosopher Vasubandhu both began their careers as Hinayana monks and later went over to the Mahayana school. However, these men belong to the period when the Mahayana movement was developing and systematizing its vast body of doctrine.

In its initial period, there can be no doubt that the lay believers, or at least certain extraordinary ones among them such as Vimala-kirti, played a key role in the development of the movement.

Scholars have suggested that there may be some connection between the rise of the Mahayana and the passion for building stupas that swept over the laity at this time. From around the third century B.C. to the third century A.D., when India was in a period of flourishing commercial activity, it became the custom for affluent members of the Buddhist laity to construct stupas or large earthen mounds commemorating the Buddha's death as an expression of their faith.

Following the demise of the Buddha, there was a growing tendency, especially among the lay believers, to deify him, as may be seen in the attribution to him of the thirty-two distinguishing features and eighty physical characteristics, a subject which I have discussed in my earlier volume. Reflecting this tendency, stupas were raised all over the country, sometimes enshrining relics of the Buddha or of eminent monks, and ceremonies of worship carried out around them. Such practices differed from those traditionally associated with the Theravadins and their derivative sects, and it has therefore been suggested that they are a manifestation of the early Mahayana movement. The surmise is that the stupas in time came to include living quarters for monks in attendance on them and that these monks constituted the beginning of the Mahayana Order.

As may be seen from the above review, there were various interrelated factors that in time appear to have led to the rise of the Mahayana movement. But we are dealing with events of two thousand or more years ago, for which only the scantiest kind of documentation exists, and we cannot hope, at this stage in our knowledge at least, to determine which factors were decisive or just how they were related to one another. The point we must not lose sight of is that the Mahayana movement did, as a matter of incontrovertible historical fact, arise at this time, and before long came to outshine the Hinayana in popularity and influence.

85

Differences between the Mahayana and Hinayana Schools

I would like next to review some of the points in which the Mahayana and Hinayana schools are generally regarded as differing. In doing so, I hope also to throw somewhat more light upon the riddle of the origin of the Mahayana movement than I was able to in the preceding section.

Scholars have already pointed out a number of ways in which the two schools of Buddhism differ. Here I would like to borrow from Dr. Hiromoto Mizuno his list of six points of difference between the *Abhidharma* or Hinayana school and the Mahayana school in its initial period and to use these as the basis for my discussion.

The first point of difference, already mentioned earlier, is that the Hinayana had as its objective the attainment of the state of arhat or saint, the goal to be attained through the so-called way of the *shōmon* or *shravaka*, the disciple who either hears the Buddha's teachings in person or who diligently follows the Four Noble Truths and the Eightfold Path. In contrast to this, the Mahayana had as its objective the attainment of Buddhahood, a goal that could be obtained by observing the practices of the bodhisattva. Let us see exactly just what this means in terms of ideals and ways of life.

The monks of the Hinayana as a whole regarded the Buddha as existing on an incomparably higher level than themselves, one which they could not possibly hope to attain, and so they confined their efforts to the attainment of the relatively less exalted level of the arhat, the "perfect being." This view seems to have been a particular characteristic of the Buddhist Order in its earliest stages, and for this reason the monks of the Order concentrated upon the practice of the Four Noble Truths and the Eightfold Path, the basic philosophical and ethical principles of Buddhism as preached by Shakyamuni shortly after his enlightenment.

But even the level of arhat was considered to be very difficult to attain, and no matter how intensively one might devote oneself to religious practices, the chances of reaching true sainthood during one's lifetime were very slight. Man is a creature of desires, and even the most pious are constantly in danger of succumbing to temptation.

Because of this outlook, the members of the Hinayana sects hedged their lives about with a great number of rules and regula-

86

tions, until their attention became wholly fixed upon matters of monastic discipline and the original aim of Buddhism, the bringing of salvation to all people, was entirely neglected. Moreover, though the goal of these early sects was to attain the stage of arhat, after the Buddha had passed away there seemed to be no certain way of determining who had actually reached that goal, and controversy broke out as to the exact nature of the arhat and the proofs of his arhatship, as in the so-called "Five Facts" concerning the arhat put forward by the monk Mahadeva of the Mahasanghika school.

In contrast, the Mahayana followers announced in effect that, without bothering with the stage of arhatship, they would set their sights upon attaining nothing short of Buddhahood. After all, they reasoned, Shakyamuni was not the only Buddha. So long as a man, any man, carried out the practices of a bodhisattva in the same way that Shakyamuni had before he reached enlightenment, then he too should be able to reach enlightenment. In the Buddhist Order as it existed in the centuries immediately after Shakyamuni's death, this represented a truly astounding and revolutionary departure in thinking.

What, according to this way of thinking, are the practices of a bodhisattva that will lead one to enlightenment? They are customarily defined in terms of the six *paramitas* or acts conducive to enlightenment, namely, donation, keeping of the precepts, perseverance, assiduity, meditation, and wisdom. Of these the most important is *dana* or donation, known in Japanese as *fuse*. But here the term does not have what was later to become its common meaning, that of the giving of donations of money and goods to the members of the Buddhist Order. The meaning is quite the opposite, a donation made by the bodhisattva to the suffering masses of humanity in the form of the Dharma. In effect, the bodhisattva goes out among the people to preach the truths of the Buddhist religion, employing the methods of *shakubuku* or *shoju*, depending upon which is appropriate to the occasion. It is important to understand the meaning of the word donation in this context, lest one imagine the bodhisattva as a person who, while preaching about the six *paramitas*, is in truth only interested in squeezing contributions out of the lay believers.

While we are on the question of terminology, let us examine the exact meaning of the word *bodhisattva*. The philosopher Nagarjuna in his *Mahaprajna-paramitopadesha* or *Daichido-ron* defines it as follows: "Because the bodhisattva in his heart profits himself and profits others; because he saves all sentient beings; because he understands the true nature of the myriad dharmas; because he carries out the way of perfect enlightenment; and because he is praised by all the saints and sages; therefore he is called 'bodhisattva.' "

The Sanskrit word *bodhisattva* has come into Japanese as *bodaisatta*, and is customarily abbreviated as *bosatsu*. Elsewhere in the *Mahaprajna-paramitopadesha* the following simple and lucid definition of the word is given: "One who seeks the Way of the Buddha in order to free all sentient beings from birth, old age, and death is called a bodhisattva."

The point to be noted in these definitions is that the bodhisattva does not strive to benefit himself alone. Rather he seeks out the Buddha Way in order to be able to save all other beings. In this respect he differs essentially from the Hinayana ideals of the *shōmon* or *shravaka* and the *engaku* or *pratyeka-buddha*, both beings who are interested primarily in their own benefit and salvation.

The *Mahaprajna-paramitopadesha* goes on to define the qualifications of the bodhisattva in these words: "He takes the Great Vow, he does not allow his heart to be moved, and he never falters in his religious practices. Because of these three factors, he is called a bodhisattva."

The Great Vow is the vow the bodhisattva takes to bring salvation to all sentient beings. The taking of this vow, along with absolute firmness of purpose and an unflagging pursuit of religious practices, therefore, constitute the three conditions necessary to qualify one as a bodhisattva.

Let us turn now to the second point in which, according to Dr. Mizuno, the *Abhidharma* or Hinayana differs from early Mahayana Buddhism. He defines it in terms of a difference between the emphasis upon karmic law, characteristic of the Hinayana, and that upon *gangyō* or "vow and practice," characteristic of the Mahayana. The former is an essentially negative attitude, which seeks to escape from the suffering imposed by karma and transmigration by fleeing to another realm. The latter is a positive approach, which deliberately seeks to encounter suffering in order to fulfill the vow and practice of the bodhisattva and to attain Buddhahood.

This is a very important point of difference. Shakyamuni, of course, taught that existence is marked by suffering, but that is not the sum of his message. He went on to urge men not to try to escape from the sufferings of birth, old age, sickness, and death, but to face up to them boldly and in that way to overcome them. This, it seems to me, is the essential message of Buddhism.

Let me put it another way. There are two attitudes one may adopt with regard to the suffering imposed by human existence. One is to look upon it as being brought about by the law of karma, thus as something that binds and torments us. This is the attitude of the Hinayana followers, who endeavor, by cutting off delusions and breaking free from the world of transmigration and suffering, to reach a realm that is peaceful and free of pain. Therefore they work to attain the goal of nirvana, a state of peace and annihilation in which one is no longer subject to rebirth. Such persons may be said to look upon human life as something predetermined and imposed upon the individual by forces beyond his control.

By contrast, Mahayana followers look upon the sufferings of human existence as something which they have willfully vowed to undergo in order to assist others to attain salvation. They do not try to escape from the world of suffering but instead deliberately thrust themselves into the most painful and degrading circumstances within that world so that they may take upon themselves the sufferings of all sentient beings. The famous lay believer Vimalakirti expressed this sense of mission of the bodhisattva when he said, "Because all sentient beings are sick, therefore I too am sick." The Hinayana attitude is passive and looks upon the conditions of life as imposed from the outside, but the approach of the bodhisattva is active and endeavors to impose its own conditions upon life.

The third point of difference pointed out by Dr. Mizuno is that, while the Hinayana aims for the improvement and advancement of the individual, the Mahayana aims for the improvement of society as a whole and for the salvation of all beings. This is a point already touched upon a number of times in our previous discussion and need not be discussed further here. We may only note that the terms *Mahayana* and *Hinayana* give symbolic expression to this point of difference, Mahayana meaning the "Great Vehicle," which conveys all sentient beings to salvation, Hinayana the "Lesser Vehicle," which is suitable only for the salvation of the single individual.

Needless to say, this terminology, expressive as it is, was the sole invention of the Mahayana school, which applied it to the earlier sects of Buddhism in the face of strong objections on their part. They attempted to retaliate, proclaiming that "Mahayana is not true Buddhism," but by this time the Mahayana movement had gained momentum and opposition proved ineffectual.

From what has been said so far, it is easy to see why the Mahayana teachings should have had great popular appeal, and it would seem that the mass of lay believers responded to them with enthusiasm and support. Thus the Mahayana school was able to override the criticisms and attacks of the older sects and to rise to a position of dominance in Indian Buddhism.

Dr. Mizuno's fourth point of difference concerns the fact that the *Abhidharma* Buddhists on the whole placed great emphasis upon the exact wording of the scriptures and were scrupulously literal in their interpretation, while the Mahayana followers favored a much freer and more creative approach. The Hinayana sects, in their formalistic approach, expended great effort in the compiling of commentaries and exegetical works on the philological meaning of the text, works which came to be known collectively as the *Abhidharma*. The Mahayana followers, on the other hand, refusing to be bound by the literal meaning of the scriptures, insisted upon a more fluid and multidimensional approach and attempted to return to what they believed to be the original spirit of Buddhism as taught by Shakyamuni and to the interpretation of the canonical writings in the light of that spirit.

Both approaches have their advantages and disadvantages, and even in modern scholarship there is dispute as to which should be adopted. Textual discussions that lose sight of the life and reality underlying the text will naturally tend to become hopelessly engrossed in minute questions of philological interpretation. On the other hand, this does not excuse one from the necessity of making a careful and thorough study of the texts. The important point is to seek always to discover the basic spirit that informs them, and when one has determined this, to ask how that spirit can be translated into action in terms of present day reality. This, it seems to me, is the necessary approach if scholarship and philosophy are to be creative.

The fifth difference between the *Abhidharma* school and the early Mahayana is directly related to the one described above. The *Abhidharma*, as we might expect, tended to be largely theoretical and pedantic in direction, and at times to wander off into idle philosophical speculation completely divorced from questions of practice. By contrast, the Mahayana in its early period valued faith and religious practice over theory and learning and insisted that any theories that may be set forth must be founded upon practice rather than empty speculation.

This is a point of extreme importance and one which anyone who considers himself a religious person must attend to carefully. The Buddhism taught by Shakyamuni did not have its origin in theoretical speculation or in academic learning. As the German philosopher Karl Jaspers put it, "What the Buddha taught was not a system of epistemology but a way of salvation."

Surveying the intellectual and spiritual world of his time, Shakyamuni saw that the members of the Brahmanical class had sunk to the pursuit of theory for the sake of theory, learning for the sake of learning. This approach he rejected, and in order to overcome it, he left his home and went out among the common people. And yet the Buddhists of the *Abhidharma* school allowed themselves to become engrossed in theoretical concerns in the same way as the Brahmans whom Shakyamuni had criticized, and neglected to think about applying their theories in practice through the conversion of the populace.

It is only natural, therefore, that the Mahayana Buddhists should have called for a return to the vital and practical approach of the faith in the time of Shakyamuni. Needless to say, they criticized the *Abhidharma* school for its strong theoretical tendency, contrasting it with their own emphasis upon practice. This does not mean that they despised theory, but they did insist upon a theory that was vital and directly related to practice. And in the course of their long doctrinal disputes with the Brahmans and the members of the Hinayana sects, they succeeded in polishing and refining their theories until in the end the Mahayana emerged as more subtle and convincing in matters of doctrine than the older sects. Theory and practice are the two wheels of the cart, and the Mahayana Buddhists were careful to neglect neither.

The sixth and final point of difference between the Hinayana and Mahayana, according to Dr. Mizuno, is that the former was essentially the concern of the monk, the specialist in the field, while the latter was designed to include the laity and the populace in general in its activities.

This is hardly more than a restatement of what has already been said above and needs no further comment here. I would merely like to note that this tendency on the part of the Hinayana to make Buddhism the preserve of the specialist seems to have been based upon a feeling that there was some fundamental social or hierarchical difference between the monastic community and the laity.

This is not an arbitrary view that I myself have arrived at. The Buddhist scholar Shōson Miyamoto, for example, expressed the same feeling when he described the early sects of Buddhism as "tending toward a prejudiced and discriminatory outlook, one that is class conscious and typical of Aryan Brahmanism and of northern India in general." In other words, the Hinayana school devoted itself to the study of doctrines which it believed only monks, the specialists in the field, were capable of understanding, and by adopting such an attitude it succeeded in shutting Buddhism off from society as a whole and making it the possession of a single group. Mahayana Buddhism, on the other hand, recognized no such rigid distinction between monk and layman and instead worked to make the religion more easily accessible to the populace as a whole and to disseminate it as widely as possible.

The Buddhist Renaissance

The rise of the Mahayana movement—the Buddhist Renaissance, if you will—is one of the most remarkable events in the history of the religion. We have outlined some of the factors involved in its origin and contributing to its success. Here I would like to call attention to another important factor which abetted its popularity, the role played by Buddhist poets and outstanding leaders and religious organizations among the laity.

At the time we are dealing with, there began to appear a type of literature that seems to have been unknown in primitive Buddhism. This consists of *Jataka* or *Birth Stories*, tales in verse and prose describing the earlier existences of the Buddha when he was still a bodhisattva, and *Avadana* or legends dealing with the Buddha's disciples or outstandingly pious believers. Because they emphasize the figure of the bodhisattva, and because their purpose seems clearly to popularize Buddhist teachings, these verses and fables would appear to have originated among a class of monks other than the *Abhidharma* followers, who, as we have seen, were secluded in their monasteries and engrossed in specialist studies. The stories are written in the Pali language.

In the early Vedic period in India, Sanskrit was the language of the Aryan peoples who occupied the north. By Shakyamuni's time, however, Sanskrit had become a highly regularized and scholarly language but one spoken only among the Brahmans and members of the ruling class. The common people spoke a number of simpler languages derived from Sanskrit and known as Prakrits, among which Pali is one of the most important. Because Shakyamuni wished his teachings to become the property not of one privileged class in society but of all men in general, he employed the simple spoken language of the people in whatever region he visited and insisted that his disciples do the same. Thus Pali, one of the common dialects of the time, rather than Sanskrit, is the language in which the early Buddhist scriptures are written.

The same desire to reach out to the common people which had motivated Shakyamuni to employ everyday speech in his teachings also inspired the composition of the *Jataka* verses and tales we have mentioned above. They represent an attempt to present the ideas of Buddhism in terms that were lively and easy for the ordinary listener to understand. In the great Mahayana scriptures such as the Lotus Sutra, which we will be discussing in detail later on, the same aim is apparent in the frequent use of parables and other literary forms designed to make the text interesting and meaningful to the layman. The *gathas* or verse portions scattered throughout these works are an obvious example.

Here it may be noted that the Indo-Aryan languages, such as Sanskrit and the dialects derived from it, are particularly suited for oral recitation. The early religious works of Brahmanism, such as the Vedic hymns, were constantly chanted and in the early centuries were handed down entirely by oral transmission. Even today, the recitations of the famous epic poem *Ramayana*, which enjoy such popularity among the Indian people, continue to give evidence of the same trait. The peoples of Indo-Aryan derivation in India seem to have been peculiarly sensitive to the musical appeal of language. For that reason, any thinker who hoped to spread his ideas among the populace would customarily cast them in poetic form, thereby giving them artistic appeal and at the same time making them easier to commit to memory.

Any system of thought, it seems to me, if it is to possess strength and vitality, must be capable of being presented to people in a genuinely interesting and enjoyable way. Needless to say, in order to gain a correct understanding of the profound philosophical principles that underlie Buddhism one must advance beyond the more popular works and master the technical treatises designed for the specialist. But to insure that Buddhism gains a true hold upon the hearts of the common people, it is imperative that it should also be able to present its teachings in a form that they take pleasure in listening to. In this sense the parables of the Buddhist scriptures, the solemn ceremonies, the hymns and rhymed verses represent practical means utilized by early Indian Buddhism in its efforts to capture the hearts of the populace.

Unfortunately, in Japan today the Buddhist scriptures are not presented to the people in a language that they can understand. Instead the ancient Chinese translations of the scriptures are simply intoned in Sino-Japanese pronunciation, so that scarcely anyone but the specialist can follow even the gist of what is being said. Sad to say, the very word for a Buddhist scripture, *okyō*, has in Japanese come to be a synonym for something incomprehensible.

In recent years we have seen a modest boom in books pertaining to Buddhism in Japan, and publishers have brought out works on the doctrines of the various sects and editions of the scriptures provided with detailed notes and commentary. This is highly commendable, but it seems to me it has gone about as far as it can go. What we need now is an outstanding literary figure who can translate the ideals and philosophical principles of Buddhism into the form and language best suited for the minds and hearts of modern Japanese. The same applies to the other countries and peoples of the world: wherever Buddhism is transmitted, it should be presented in the form most compatible with the tastes and temperaments of the people to whom it is addressed, though I realize that this may take many years to accomplish.

But to return to the India of two thousand years ago, one final point remains, that of whether there existed an organization of lay Buddhist believers, as distinct from the monastic orders of the various Hinayana sects.

I am strongly inclined to think that such an organization did exist, though we must await further study before we can attempt to say just what form it had. The Vimalakirti Sutra (discussed in the next chapter) centers around a highly enlightened and influential lay believer named Vimalakirti. Some scholars would view him as a purely fictitious figure, an embodiment of the ideal layman, but I wonder if he did not have his real-life models among the outstanding lay leaders of the Buddhist community. And I wonder if the Vimalakirti Sutra and works like it are not in fact the product of some kind of formal group or religious organization, though probably not one as tightly knit as the Sangha or Buddhist Order itself.

The Lotus Sutra as well, as we shall have occasion to discuss later, would seem to have been transmitted by a group or organization of highly enlightened laymen, who at times encountered considerable pressure from outside. Of course such organizations did not consist of laymen alone. They undoubtedly included monks as well but looked upon both monk and layman as essentially the same. And the real leadership of the group came, I would surmise, from enlightened laymen, men who believed in the equality of all peoples and social classes and who were dedicated to the realization of the bodhisattva ideal. If some such organization had not existed in these early days, it is difficult to see how the Mahayanaists could have preserved and handed down such a large body of scriptures.

The exact organizational form of the early Mahayana, as well as the exact process by which it came into being, may, as we have seen, be clouded in historical uncertainty. Yet the fact remains: some five hundred years after the death of the Buddha, at a time when the Dharma which Shakyamuni had taught seemed almost in danger of extinction, this new movement did come to the fore in India, restoring vitality to the religion and carrying its teachings eastward through Central Asia to China and eventually to Japan. Its appearance, consequently, was of enormous significance, bringing about as it did a veritable Renaissance in Indian Buddhism, and its history is fraught with lessons of the greatest importance for us today.

7

Vimalakirti and the Ideal
of the Lay Believer

Vimalakirti

With the rise of the Mahayana movement, Buddhism underwent a process of rejuvenation. A key role in this process was played by the leaders of the lay community, and I would like therefore to consider for a moment their way of life and contribution to the early history of the Buddhist religion. This can perhaps best be accomplished by focusing upon the figure of Vimalakirti as he is described in the sutra entitled *Vimalakirti-nirdesha* or Exposition of Vimalakirti and popularly referred to as the Vimalakirti Sutra.

Vimalakirti, the rich merchant of the city of Vaishali, eloquent in speech, highly skilled in debate, of prodigious memory—he is a figure of endless fascination and mystery. Unlike the major disciples of Shakyamuni, who seem completely removed from the everyday world and almost prim in their enlightenment, he lived the kind of full and unfettered life appropriate to the true layman. He represents the complete opposite of the arhat ideal upheld by the monks of the Hinayana sects, a living embodiment of the Mahayana spirit in its rejection of narrow monasticism and its insistence that Buddhism be made to flourish throughout society as a whole.

For Buddhist believers of India, China, and Japan, particularly lay believers, Vimalakirti has been a figure of enormous popularity. This is clear from the fact that the Vimalakirti Sutra has been more widely read than any other Mahayana sutra outside of the Lotus Sutra. There were six Chinese translations made of it, of which three are still extant. Among these, the second, made by the great translator Kumarajiva (344–413), is considered the finest in literary style and has been most widely read. The philosopher Nagarjuna in his *Mahaprajna-paramitopadesha* cites the Vimalakirti Sutra more often than any text other than the Lotus, and the T'ien-t'ai school of Buddhism in China likewise regarded it as of great importance and produced a commentary on it. In Japan, it was one of the three sutras for which Prince Shōtoku wrote commentaries, the others being the Lotus and the Queen Shrimala.

It shares with the Lotus Sutra the distinction of being among the most dramatic and effective works in the Mahayana canon and has accordingly exercised a great influence upon poets and writers in China and Japan. The famous Chinese poet of the T'ang dynasty Wang Wei, for example, showed his reverence for it by adopting Vimalakirti's name as his own, his personal names Wei and Mo-chieh together forming the Chinese transliteration of the name *Vima-lakirti*. The *Hōjōki* or "Account of my Hut" by Kamo no Chōmei, a classic of early Japanese literature, is also deeply influenced by the thought of the Vimalakirti Sutra, and the "ten-foot-square hut" the author describes is modeled directly after Vimalakirti's famous *hōjō* or ten-foot-square room.

Although the great literary beauty of the text, as well as the fact that it never became associated with any one particular school of Buddhism, may account in part for its wide and lasting popularity, it seems to me that the most important factor is the fascination which Vimalakirti exerts on the reader as a human being, and the aptness with which he exemplifies the practical application of the Mahayana spirit. The text describes how Vimalakirti engaged in debate with one after another of Shakyamuni's major disciples, and repeatedly shows him getting the better of them through his incisive wit and eloquence. We even find him discoursing with Manjushri, who is known as the Bodhisattva of Supreme Wisdom, debating in masterful fashion on the most profound aspects of Mahayana philosophy.

Buddhist thought in the early period prior to the rise of the Mahayana movement, as remarked earlier, had focused on the figure of the monk, who strictly abides by the rules of discipline and tries through the teachings handed down from Shakyamuni to achieve sainthood. Vimalakirti stands in utter contrast to such monastic figures, a rich merchant, a prominent citizen of the bustling city of Vaishali, beloved by his fellow citizens and on the closest terms with them. He has a wife and family, he engages in business activities, and on occasion he is to be found in the pleasure quarters and gambling houses of the city, where he goes to preach the doctrines of Mahayana Buddhism. He is a practitioner of the Dharma such as the earlier Buddhist Order, with its emphasis upon monasticism, could scarcely have conceived of.

We have, it should be noted, no evidence outside of the sutra itself to indicate that Vimalakirti ever existed. The Chinese monk Hsüan-tsang reports that when he visited the city of Vaishali in the course of his journey to India in the seventh century, he was shown Vimalakirti's old house, as well as various locations where the famous layman was said to have preached. However, this proves very little, since numerous figures who existed only in literature or legend have similarly been provided with authentic-appearing birthplaces, dwellings, apparel, and so on. For all we know, Vimalakirti may, as some Buddhologists insist, be no more than a fictional embodiment of the ideal layman created by later followers of the Mahayana school.

There is certainly no way to refute such an assertion, for, as we have seen, Western scholars in the past frequently denied that Shakyamuni himself had ever existed, while King Ashoka, up until the discovery of the texts of his edicts, was dismissed as a legendary ruler whose exploits were the creation of pious Buddhist believers.

Even if Vimalakirti is a purely imaginary figure, this in no way diminishes the worth of the great Mahayana sutra in which his activities are described. It is not the historicity of Vimalakirti that is important, but the way in which the sutra uses him to illuminate the bodhisattva ideal, to depict the practical measures that should be taken to disseminate Buddhism throughout society as a whole, and to give expression to a profound and lofty view of existence that transcends the dualism of being and non-being. Vimalakirti is simply a vehicle for the transmission of the Mahayana spirit.

Whether Vimalakirti was a real person or a literary invention, the city of Vaishali, the scene of his activities, was no figment of the imagination. It was a thriving commercial center of northern India and an important source of support for the Mahayana movement. Shakyamuni himself had expressed great fondness for the city and had visited it with his disciples a number of times. Shortly before his death, when he set off in the direction of his old home in Kapilavastu, he stopped for a time in the city, and on leaving it, exclaimed, "How beautiful is Vaishali!" In view of this, it would not be at all surprising if there had in fact been important lay believers such as Vimalakirti living in the city at the time.

We should not imagine Shakyamuni's famous disciples as being the only ones who listened to his teachings, though their stories are recorded most fully in the early scriptures. In the early years of Shakyamuni's religious organization, he no doubt preached at great length to the group of young men who had taken up the monastic life and gathered about him. But as his fame spread and more and more people came to listen to his teachings, it is only natural to suppose that a growing number of men and women became lay followers of the new religion. The scriptures in fact record that King Bimbisara, the ruler of Magadha, as well as King Pasenadi, the ruler of Koshala, both became converts to the faith, and we are also told of converts among the wealthy merchants such as Sudatta, who donated the famous Jetavana monastery to the Order.

When Shakyamuni addressed these lay believers, we may be certain that he directed them to observe somewhat different religious practices from those ordained for the monks, and it is therefore reasonable to suppose that the doctrines he taught them differed to some extent in content from those taught to the monks. If these doctrines are in fact the ones later crystalized in the form of the Mahayana scriptures, then we may surmise that they emphasized the duty of the Buddhist believer to work for the benefit of others rather than for his own benefit and to spread the Dharma throughout society as a whole.

My own feeling is that Shakyamuni looked to the Order of monks to insure that the body of philosophical and religious doctrines that he had so fervently preached during the fifty years subsequent to his enlightenment would be handed down correctly to posterity, while he depended upon the laymen, with their active spirit and knowledge of the world, to spread his doctrines throughout society. If my supposition is correct, then we may say that Shakyamuni in his teaching recognized both the monks and the laity as of equal importance and saw each as performing a distinctive and indispensable function.

The Building of a Buddha Land

Let us look for a moment at Kumarajiva's three-section translation of the Vimalakirti Sutra, which is known in Japanese as the

Yuimakitsu-shosetsu-gyō, and see what kind of person Vimalakirti was.

The first section, which comprises the first four chapters of the work, deals with events that took place in the gardens of Ambapali in the suburbs of the city of Vaishali. Ambapali was a courtesan of Vaishali and a woman of deep religious faith. In India at this time, courtesans and prostitutes were supervised and protected by the state. Ambapali was looked upon as one of the prize possessions of Vaishali, being not only beautiful but highly intelligent and cultured as well. She was very wealthy and owned lovely gardens in the suburbs, which she presented to Shakyamuni as a token of her faith. For this reason, he and his followers always stayed at the gardens when he had occasion to visit Vaishali. In the episode described in the Vimalakirti Sutra, Shakyamuni has come to visit and, accompanied by eight thousand monks and thirty-two hundred bodhisattvas, is resting under the mango trees.

At this point a young man named Hōshaku appears leading a company of five hundred young noblemen of the city of Vaishali, each carrying a parasol decorated with the seven types of precious objects, to visit Shakyamuni. Thereupon, we are told, Shakyamuni made the five hundred parasols into a single parasol, with which he shaded the worlds of the three thousand realms. The episode can be taken to mean that the individual egos of the five hundred noblemen are negated in favor of the single great ego of the Buddha. Underlying the passage is the kind of thinking that elsewhere finds expression in the concept of *ichinen-sanzen* or the three thousand realms as contained in one moment of existence.

Hōshaku, who is filled with awe by the Buddha's presence, proceeds to recite a hymn of praise to the World Honored One. In it appears the famous passage:

"The Buddha expounds the Dharma with a single voice,
but each being understands it according to his own kind."

The meaning is that each person listening to an exposition of Buddhist principles will understand them in a somewhat different way depending upon his own nature and capacity. No matter how eloquently the Dharma may be expounded, if the listener has only the narrow outlook of a person in the *shōmon* or *engaku* category, he cannot comprehend the Buddha's teachings of the Mahayana. On the other hand, if he has the breadth of mind that can think in terms of the three thousand realms, then he will experience no difficulty in grasping the Buddha's true meaning. The passage is a reminder of how important it is that we who seek the Dharma should do so with an attitude of broadmindedness and receptivity.

Hōshaku then asks Shakyamuni what the bodhisattva should do in order to create or establish Buddha lands of complete purity. Shakyamuni replies to the question as follows: "Hōshaku, the lands of all sentient beings are the Buddha lands of the bodhisattva just as they are! Why? Because Buddha lands are maintained by the beings who have been converted by the bodhisattva, and they are maintained by the beings who have been brought to submission by the bodhisattva. Buddha lands are enlarged by the entry of various beings into the wisdom of the Buddha, and they are enlarged when men awake in themselves the nature proper to a bodhisattva. Thus the Buddha lands of the bodhisattva are all designed to benefit sentient beings."

The bodhisattva works to create realms or Buddha lands marked by perfect purity, but as the passage here makes clear, these "Buddha lands" are not some distant "Pure Land" of the west. They exist already within the spirit of the bodhisattva when he takes a vow to bring benefit to all sentient beings and actively works for the realization of such lands. In other words, the Buddha land is to be seen not as a result to be achieved but as the impetus to, or the process of, achieving it. This is a good example of the dynamic quality typical of the Vimalakirti Sutra as a whole. The passage may also be read as a formula for measuring the area over which one's propagation of the Dharma can effectively spread. That is to say, when a practitioner of the faith is preaching to the persons of a certain region, the degree to which he understands his own mission as a bodhisattva to convert men through the teachings of the Mahayana, to lead them into the realm of the Buddha's wisdom, and to bring salvation to all beings will determine just how pure and far-reaching is the Buddha land he creates.

The episodes described above all occur in the first chapter of the sutra, that entitled "Buddha Lands." With the second chapter, "Expedient Means," we catch our first glimpse of the remarkable Vimalakirti. *Vimala* in Sanskrit means "undefiled," and *kirti* means "fame" or "reputation." Hsüan-tsang, in his translation of the sutra, renders the name as Mukushō or "Renowned as Undefiled," but Kumarajiva simply employs Chinese characters to indicate the Sanskrit pronunciation. Because of the fame of the Kumarajiva translation, Vimalakirti has commonly come to be referred to as Yuimakitsu or simply Yuima in China and Japan. Nichiren Dai-shōnin in the *Gosho* customarily refers to him by the name Jōmyō, which means "Famed for Purity" and is hence a translation of the Sanskrit name, and refers to the sutra as the *Jōmyō-gyō*, though on occasion he also uses the names Yuima and *Yuima-gyō*.

The text tells us that there was a rich man of Vaishali known as Vimalakirti or "Renowned as Undefiled," a lay believer of Bud-dhism who was skilled in employing a variety of expedient means to convert people to the teachings of the faith.

According to the sutra, he was a man of varied activities. His business ventures prospered, and he is said to have taken pains to spread the profits he received among the populace at large. He went all about the city of Vaishali giving guidance to the people, visited the schools and instructed the children in a skillful manner, and had a wide range of friends among both old and young. He was also well acquainted with the popular writings of the time, and was well liked by the officials and members of the Brahman class.

"If he were among the high officials," the scripture tells us, "he would teach the true Dharma in a manner befitting the most honor-able of the high officials." Perhaps he had in fact at one time served as a high official; since Vaishali had a republican form of govern-ment, it is quite possible that he had been selected to hold some important post. In any event, he was one of the outstanding citizens of the state.

Vimalakirti's position in Vaishali reminds us in some ways of that of Socrates in Athens, except, of course, that Socrates was by no means wealthy. And if Vimalakirti enjoyed greater affluence than Socrates, he was also more fortunate than the latter in the reception given to him by his fellow citizens. This was amply demonstrated on the famous occasion of his illness, when kings, high officials, elders, lay believers, Brahmans, princes, and various other officials, numbering several thousand persons in all, came to inquire about his health. Such was the love and affection he enjoyed.

Shakyamuni was at the time staying in Ambapali's gardens, and he too decided to send someone to call on Vimalakirti. The third and fourth chapters of the sutra, entitled "The Disciples" and "The Bodhisattvas" respectively, describe how Shakyamuni designates one after another of his Ten Major Disciples, followed by Maitreya and three other bodhisattvas, to undertake the mission. But each person as he is designated recalls how in the past he has been bested by Vimalakirti in some manner and declares himself unfit to undertake the mission.

To give an example, Shariputra, who was known among the major disciples as "foremost in wisdom," relates how he was once sitting cross-legged in meditation under a tree when Vimalakirti appeared and began to lecture him on the proper method of sitting in meditation. "Shariputra," he said, "sitting is not necessarily sitting in meditation. Sitting in meditation means that you do not show your body or mind in the Three Worlds. It also means displaying your majesty in a natural manner in the state in which body and mind have been annihilated. It means being able to search for the Buddha Way at the same time that you carry on in an exemplary manner the daily activities of the world. This is what is called sitting in meditation."

Shariputra, addressed in this fashion, was unable to think of any reply and could only remain seated in silence. Because of this experience, he explains to Shakyamuni that he is unable to undertake the task of calling upon Vimalakirti to inquire of his health.

These passages present an attack upon the disciples of Shakyamuni and their Hinayana views and practices from the point of view of the Mahayana. Thus, as in the example just quoted, the Hinayana practices are criticized for the formalism into which they had fallen, and emphasis is placed instead upon the content and actual effectiveness of the practice. The typical Mahayana spirit is very much in evidence here.

It is interesting to note that each of the Ten Major Disciples is made to come forward in this manner and confess his inability to measure up to Vimalakirti, the ideal of the Mahayana bodhisattva. The text at this point is very vivid and dramatic. Unfortunately, however, in its zeal to attack the *shōmon* and *engaku* ideals of the Hinayana, it sometimes allows itself to go beyond the bounds of reason. Thus, for example, Shariputra is from first to last in the Vimalakirti Sutra treated as a kind of clown. In matter of fact, however, we know that he was anything but a clown, in real life playing a very important role, along with the other major disciples, in the leadership of the religious organization founded by Shakyamuni.

Nichiren Daishōnin writes in the *Gosho*: "This work called the Vimalakirti Sutra is only a minor retainer far down the line from

103

the Lotus Sutra." In other words, because the Vimalakirti never advanced beyond the stage of criticizing the Hinayana, it never came anywhere near the lofty level represented by the Lotus Sutra. The Vimalakirti Sutra therefore serves only as a kind of introduction to the Lotus, which is probably what Nichiren Daishōnin means by calling it a "retainer."

Some scholars see the Vimalakirti and the Lotus as belonging to the same "family" of Mahayana works. But Vimalakirti, whom one would expect to be above such preoccupation with distinctions, appears obsessed with the differences between the Hinayana ideals of the *shōmon* and *engaku* and the Mahayana ideal of the bodhisattva. This inability to transcend such distinctions constitutes the main flaw in the Vimalakirti Sutra.

How the Bodhisattva Benefits Others

The second section of Kumarajiva's translation, which comprises chapters five to nine, takes us to the *hōjō* or "ten-foot-square" sickroom of Vimalakirti. It has been decided that the bodhisattva Manjushri shall undertake on Shakyamuni's behalf to inquire about Vimalakirti's illness. He is accompanied by eight thousand bodhisattvas, five hundred *shōmon* or *shravaka* disciples, and one hundred thousand devas or heavenly beings. All are certain that any exchange between Manjushri and Vimalakirti will be well worth listening to, and they crowd around in excitement and anticipation.

The room where Vimalakirti lies awaiting them is bare except for a bed and measures only one *jō* or about ten feet on each side. And yet, strange to say, the entire crowd of visitors is able to fit into it. This is something that the ordinary rationalist might find difficult to understand and accept.

Shariputra too, we are told in chapter six, was puzzled by the phenomenon, whereupon Vimalakirti said to him: "Shariputra! In the enlightenment attained by the various Buddhas and bodhisattvas there is a doctrine called the Mysterious. If as a bodhisattva one enters into this enlightenment, then Mount Sumeru, huge and vast as it is, can be placed inside a tiny mustard seed without anything being left over. Moreover, the outlook from Mount Sumeru will remain unchanged, and the guardian deities of the four quarters and the thirty-three gods who dwell on the mountain will be unaware that they have entered into a mustard seed. Only those who are even more enlightened than they are can understand that Mount Sumeru has entered into a mustard seed. This is called the doctrine of the Solving of the Mystery."

The passage is in effect an exposition of the Mahayana doctrine of *shunyata* or the "void." The conversations between Manjushri and Vimalakirti also are based upon this concept of emptiness or the state that is empty of, or beyond, any characteristic by which it might be described. In chapter nine, entitled "Entering the Doctrine of the Non-Dual," this concept is discussed from various angles, being described as "not existing and yet not not existing, not coming into being and yet not going out of being, not acting and yet not not acting." It is the non-dualism that is incapable of being understood in ordinary terms, the realm of absolute monism.

It is this realm that the bodhisattva seeks through various practices to reach. But let us see now what those practices consist of. To do so, we return to Vimalakirti as he is described in chapter five, entitled "Inquiring about the Illness." Manjushri, appearing at the bedside of Vimalakirti, asks about the nature of his illness. Vimalakirti replies in the famous words that follow:

"In my stupidity I have developed a sense of love, and it is from this that my sickness arises. Because all beings are sick, therefore I am sick. If the sickness of the beings were to go away, then my sickness would go away. Why? Because the bodhisattva enters the realm of birth and death for the sake of other beings. Since there is birth and death, there must be sickness. If other beings could free themselves from sickness, then the bodhisattva too would no longer be sick. It is like the only child of a rich man. If the child is sick, then the father and mother too will be sick, but if the child recovers, then the father and mother too will recover. It is the same with the bodhisattva. He loves all beings as though they were his children. If they are sick, then the bodhisattva too will be sick, but if they recover, then the bodhisattva too will recover. You ask me, 'What is the cause from which this sickness arises?' The sickness of the bodhisattva arises from his great compassion."

From this it becomes apparent that Vimalakirti's illness, rather than being due to any physical disorder, is mental and spiritual in nature. It is common enough to remark that a person in good health cannot even understand the sufferings of someone who is sick. Here, however, we are presented with a task that is even more difficult: to not only understand but to share in the sufferings of others and to make them our own. The Buddha is described as suffering from sickness and illusion, though to a much lesser degree than ordinary beings. This is because he shares in the sufferings and illusions of other beings and makes them his own.

The followers of the Hinayana, however, had lost sight of the spirit of the original teachings of Shakyamuni and had become concerned only with seeking the perfection of their own religious practices. Therefore the Mahayana arose with its opposite view to counterpose this, the ideal of the bodhisattva who seeks to attain Buddhahood by benefiting others. In order to do so, he must first of all place himself in the position where he shares in the sufferings of other beings.

Vimalakirti then goes on to describe the practices of the bodhisattva in the following way: "Though he looks upon the various Buddha lands as eternal and free from birth and death, still he works to make them manifest in all their purity to other beings— this is the practice of the bodhisattva. Though he seeks the way of the Buddha, preaches the Dharma, and enters the realm of nirvana, still he does not abandon his pursuits as a bodhisattva—this too is the practice of the bodhisattva."

Upon hearing these words of Vimalakirti, we are told, eight thousand of the heavenly beings who had accompanied Manjushri attained the realm of unsurpassed enlightenment.

The point of the passage is to make clear that the bodhisattva, while working to perfect his own religious practices, also labors to bring about the creation of "Buddha lands" or ideal worlds within the actual society of the time in which he lives. Unlike the Hinayana follower who, in pursuit of the arhat ideal, strives only to free himself from pain and delusion, he exists upon a higher level of understanding of the Dharma, and upon this level labors unremittingly to create Buddha lands for the sake of all beings. This is the lofty mission that Mahayana philosophy assigns to the bodhisattva.

Upon the conclusion of this eloquent and penetrating dialogue between Vimalakirti and Manjushri concerning the nature of the bodhisattva, a devi or goddess who was a member of Vimalakirti's household suddenly appears and scatters heavenly flowers over the assembly. The flowers which land on the bodhisattvas fall immediately to the ground, but those which land on the *shōmon* or *shravaka* disciples all stick tightly to them. Shariputra and the other disciples of Shakyamuni begin frantically trying to brush off the flowers, but they refuse to come off.

The goddess, laughing, asks Shariputra, "Why do you try to pull the flowers off?"

Shariputra replies, "Goddess, I am trying to pull them off because such flowers are not appropriate on the person of a monk!"

But the goddess is quite capable of holding her own in a debate with Shariputra, the "foremost in wisdom" among Shakyamuni's disciples. She proceeds to point out that the flowers themselves have no such preconceptions as to what is appropriate or not. It is precisely because Shariputra and the other *shravaka* disciples still harbor preconceptions and remnants of discriminatory thinking that the flowers stick to them. For the practitioner of the Way who is still in fear of the cycle of transmigration, each of the senses of sight, smell, sound, taste, and touch will become a source of delusion, an opening whereby the devil may get at him.

It is clear that the goddess has been victorious in this first encounter. Shariputra, however, unwisely decides to taunt her with her sex. "Goddess," he asks her, "why don't you change out of your female form?"

The goddess replies by using her magical powers to transform Shariputra into female form, much to his horror and consternation, while she herself takes on Shariputra's form.

Once again the same point is made: Shariputra, who represents the viewpoint of the Hinayana, cannot free himself from the type of thinking that insists upon assigning things to hard and fast categories. Yet from the point of view of the Dharma, which recognizes the equality of all beings, it is all the same whether one is a man or a woman. As the goddess says, quoting the words of Shakyamuni, "In the equality of all beings, there is neither man nor woman." The thinking in the whole passage, incidentally, is close to that seen in chapter twelve of the Lotus Sutra where the dragon king's daughter is transformed into a man and attains Buddhahood.

One final point to note in these episodes is the intensity with which those who come into contact with Vimalakirti devoted themselves to the search for enlightenment. Where there is a lay believer of such deep faith and understanding as Vimalakirti, he is bound to inspire devotion in all who are associated with him.

The Doctrine of the Mysterious

The Vimalakirti Sutra is customarily praised for the superbly dramatic construction of the text, and certainly the amusing exchange between the goddess and Shariputra, which we have just described, constitutes a remarkable comic interlude within the larger drama of the sutra. In chapter eight, entitled "The Buddha Way," Vimalakirti and Manjushri concentrate their heated discussions upon the question of the nature of the enlightenment of the Buddha, while in chapter nine, "Entering the Doctrine of the Non-Dual," the thirty-two bodhisattvas explore the nature of this so-called doctrine of non-dualism from various angles.

This is generally regarded as the high point of the sutra, for it contains the famous "silence of Vimalakirti, which is like a clap of thunder." One by one, the bodhisattvas set forth their respective opinions concerning the nature of the doctrine of non-dualism. But when it comes Vimalakirti's turn to present his answer to the problem, he merely sits silent without speaking a word. Thus he indicates by his attitude that the realm of the non-dual is and always has been above and beyond all words, a place where all workings of the mind come to an end.

Manjushri, filled with admiration at Vimalakirti's reply, exclaims "Excellent! excellent! This is the true entry of the bodhisattva into the doctrine of the non-dual, where there is no written or spoken word." We are told that the five thousand bodhisattvas assembled on the spot at the time thereupon achieved the stage of enlightenment known as *mushōhōnin*, one of the higher stages of enlightenment.

The last section of the sutra, which comprises chapters ten to fourteen, deals with a Buddha named Kōshaku or Accumulation of Fragrance who presides over Shukōkoku, the Land of All Fragrances, and preaches the Dharma by means of various wonderful perfumes.

As the discussions between Vimalakirti and Manjushri rambled on, the sutra relates, it grew to be almost noontime and Shariputra began to worry about lunch. According to the rules of discipline observed by the monks of the period, it was forbidden to take any food after the noon hour had passed. It is ironic that Shariputra, who had entered the monastic order so as to free himself from worldly cares and delusions, should still be worried about his lunch, though at the same time one cannot help feeling a bond of human sympathy with him. Vimalakirti, noticing his restlessness, asked, "Do you think you can listen to the Dharma while you are worrying about food?" It was not the kindest remark, but Vimalakirti went on to add, "If you want something to eat, wait a moment. I will give you such food as you have never tasted before!" He thereupon sent for a meal of scents from the Land of All Fragrances. The messenger whom Vimalakirti dispatched to the Land of All Fragrances found himself, we are told, in a realm where no written or spoken words are employed, but the Dharma is preached entirely through the means of various scents. There are no *shōmon* or *engaku* disciples in the realm, men whose understanding is still limited to the level of the Hinayana; it is inhabited entirely by bodhisattvas of the highest degree of purity, who are able to subsist on fragrances alone.

The Land of All Fragrances, in spite of its fairy-story qualities, is described with great vividness, and we see here the immense imaginative powers of the writers of the Mahayana scriptures. Because they looked upon the Dharma as something that could unlock and explain the mysteries of the life force, they felt that it should be presented in terms of realms or visions transcending ordinary human imagination. Thus, to describe the Dharma as being expounded not in words but in beautiful fragrances is a way of jarring the mind into an awareness of its transcendental nature.

The passage also goes on to make clear that, seen from the Land of All Fragrances, our present world is a place of evil and corruption, full of beings who are crabbed in spirit and bent upon pursuing the meanest goals, thus making it extremely difficult for the Buddhas and bodhisattvas to save them. For this very reason, the Buddhas are forced to preach the Dharma in words rather than in fragrances, and the bodhisattvas must deliberately take on existence in the lower realms of being in order to fight fiercely and unrelentingly to overcome evil.

Vimalakirti, when told this by the bodhisattvas of the Land of All Fragrances, replied that the bodhisattvas of our present world possess "ten types of goodness." These consist of various practices that are to be carried out, the main ones being the six paramitas, that is, donation, the keeping of the precepts, perseverance, assiduity, meditation, and wisdom. The simple list of rules or practices laid down here for the Mahayana believer is intended to form a striking contrast with the some 250 or 500 rules of discipline prescribed for the Hinayana monks.

This is followed by a list of "eight laws" that the bodhisattva carrying out religious practices in our present world is instructed to take as his model. Since these eight laws have considerable application in ethical terms for men and women in the world today, I quote the list in full.

1. Though benefiting the people of the world, you shall look for no reward.

2. You shall take upon yourself all the sufferings of all sentient beings.

3. Any merit you may acquire you shall transfer entirely to others.

4. You shall look on all people as equal and without distinction, shall humble yourself before them, and allow no impediments to arise in your mind regarding them. You shall look upon all bodhisattvas as though they were Buddhas.

5. Though hearing a sutra you have never heard before, you shall not regard it with suspicion; you shall not argue with the followers of the Hinayana.

6. You shall not be envious of the alms other men receive, nor boast of your own gains, but shall keep your mind in check.

7. You shall reflect upon your own errors, and shall not speak of the faults of others.

8. You shall at all times maintain a heart that is unmoving and shall strive to attain merit of all kinds.

It is said that if one gives himself whole-heartedly to the task of profiting others and saving the people, he will as a matter of course be able to realize these eight aims. One will note immediately that, in contrast to the minute and highly constraining rules of discipline of the Hinayana, these are in the nature of broad ethical goals that are designed to guide one's attitude and approach.

After this, the sutra returns once more to the scene of Ambapali's gardens, where the true identity of Vimalakirti is further revealed, and ends by entrusting itself to the care of Maitreya and Ananda.

Another name for the Vimalakirti Sutra is The Doctrine of the Incomprehensible Enlightenment, and certainly the figure of Vimalakirti, as presented in it, is surrounded with mysteries and wonders. He represents the ideal of the lay believer as it was formulated some two thousand years ago, and yet in a sense he is also the forerunner of our present day Soka Gakkai. Needless to say, the Soka Gakkai bases itself upon the teachings of the Lotus Sutra and therefore is under no obligation to follow the rules for religious practice laid down by Vimalakirti as outlined above. But as we come increasingly to understand the real essence and meaning of the Dharma, I believe we will find that in the end both the Lotus Sutra and the Vimalakirti Sutra point to a single truth.

8

The Formation
of the Lotus Sutra

The Preaching of the Dharma on Vulture Peak

Up to this point we have discussed the historical development of Buddhism in India in the centuries immediately following the death of Shakyamuni. We come now to a consideration of what is undoubtedly the most important text of Buddhism, the Lotus Sutra, and of the question of just how it came into existence.

Of all the vast number of texts contained in the Buddhist canon, the Lotus is generally regarded as preeminent. This is no mere partisan assertion but a view endorsed by Buddhists and non-Buddhists alike. The fact that in India, China, and Japan there are more commentaries on this text than on any other in the canon offers further proof of its enormous importance. The Chinese monk Chih-k'ai or Chih-i (538–97), the founder of the T'ien-t'ai school, devoted his entire life to the task of lecturing and writing commentaries on the text, so highly did he regard it. To do justice to such a work, of course, would require far more time and space than we can allot to it here.

Shakyamuni is said to have preached the Lotus Sutra over a period of eight years, his disciples later gathering together the sermons, and many hundreds of years passed before the text reached the form in which we have it now. The Lotus, in fact, is not only the most famous of all Mahayana sutras but represents a compendium and distillation of the entire system of Indian Buddhist philosophy as it was created by Shakyamuni.

The Lotus was in time transmitted to China, where it was translated into Chinese, and by this route became known in Japan as well, particularly in the eight section translation by Kumarajiva entitled *Miao-fa lien-hua-ching* or *Myōhō-renge-kyō*. The 69,384 characters of this text came to be looked upon as so many golden emblems of the Dharma. The Lotus Sutra has had an incalculable influence upon Japanese culture. Any number of expressions which we Japanese of modern times employ in our everyday lives derive originally from the Lotus Sutra, though in most cases we are scarcely conscious of their origin.

We must reserve for another occasion the task of examining each of the eight large sections and twenty-eight chapters of the text one by one. Here I wish to focus upon the conditions which surrounded the formation of this remarkable text in the India of two thousand years ago.

The question immediately arises as to whether, as has been asserted in recent times, the Lotus Sutra is a fabrication of Buddhist believers of later centuries. This possibility has been raised by philological studies in which it is suggested that the earliest version of the text could not have come into existence any earlier than the first century B.C., and that this original version was gradually added to until, sometime around the first century A.D., it reached the form in which we have it now. Because of this, the charge has been leveled that the Mahayana doctrines expounded in the text do not represent the real teachings of Buddhism as they were originally set forth. I find it difficult to believe, however, that the Lotus Sutra and the other Mahayana scriptures have no connection whatsoever with the teachings of Shakyamuni and are pure inventions of Mahayana followers of later ages, who simply attached the formula "Thus have I heard" on to the beginning of the texts in order to make them appear genuine.

I do not mean to suggest, of course, that all the vast number of texts in the Buddhist canon represent an exact record of the teachings of Shakyamuni just as he pronounced them. We have seen that, according to the accounts, the First Council was held shortly after Shakyamuni's death to put his teachings into order, and that for the following two or three hundred years they were handed down orally, the words being committed to memory by one generation of disciples after another. Scholars surmise that it was not until around the first century B.C. that the texts were put into written form such as we have them now. This means that the written forms of the Hinayana texts are in fact no older than the early Mahayana texts, and if the latter are to be labeled "non-Buddhist" because they have no demonstrable link with the teachings of Shakyamuni, then the same may be said of such basic Hinayana texts as the *Agama* or *Agon* sutras.

The important point to keep in mind here, it seems to me, is not the findings of philology but the fact that the works of the Buddhist canon, including both Hinayana and Mahayana texts, have traditionally been read as expositions of the Dharma and as such have become a living part of the religious and philosophical thought of the peoples of Asia. It is this living and viable quality in them that constitutes the essence of the religion. Therefore I believe it is proper to regard them as the product of careful and intense effort made by the early disciples to hand down the teachings of Shakyamuni just as he revealed them over the fifty-year period following his enlightenment. This thesis philology can neither prove nor disprove, and we should not allow its carpings to distract us from the far more important consideration of the content of these writings.

Here we face a problem that has troubled students of Buddhism and the Buddhist texts down through the ages, that of why, if these are in essence the teachings of Shakyamuni, they should at times appear to differ and even contradict each other. In attempting to explain the differences and contradictions, we should keep the following considerations in mind.

First is the fact that, in the course of fifty years of preaching, we may naturally surmise that there was a certain degree of change and progression in the way in which Shakyamuni presented his ideas. He achieved enlightenment under the Bodhi tree in Buddha-gaya and thereafter preached his first sermon at the Deer Park in Benares. But is it reasonable to suppose that he then went on repeating the very same sermon day after day, year after year? I hardly think so. Though the fundamentals of the enlightenment he had achieved remained the same, he must repeatedly have turned over in his mind the question of how best to explain his experience and its meaning to the populace as a whole. No doubt wisdom dictated that he explain it in a number of somewhat different ways depending upon the circumstances under which he was preaching.

First of all, he undoubtedly took into consideration the capacities of his listeners at any particular time and adjusted his discourse accordingly. And even when addressing a single individual, such as one of his close disciples, it is only natural to suppose that Shakyamuni changed the content of his preaching as the disciple progressed in spiritual training, gradually leading him step by step into the deeper mysteries of the Dharma. Thus he took the utmost care to guide the members of his new Order, nourishing and encouraging the individual capacities of each until in the end all had reached the stage of Buddhahood.

We must consider the influence which the gradual growth and development of the Buddhist Order must have had upon the method and content of Shakyamuni's teachings.

Shakyamuni began his preaching career as a single individual challenging the intellectual world of ancient India. He appears at first to have directed his discourse mainly toward ascetics who were engaged in the practice of various religious austerities, refuting the views of the Brahmans and the so-called six unorthodox teachers or freethinkers, and presenting his own system of thought founded upon the profound enlightenment he himself had achieved. As the number of ascetics who responded to his doctrines increased, they in time came to form the Buddhist Order, and Shakyamuni accordingly laid down certain doctrines and rules for the guidance and discipline of the group. These early teachings, we may suppose, in the years after his death took shape in what eventually were to become the *Agama* sutras. Certainly the *Agama* sutras are vitally concerned with questions of monastic discipline and are often fragmentary in content, suggesting that they represent a collection of various instructions given by Shakyamuni to his immediate disciples for their specific guidance.

As Shakyamuni's fame spread, persons other than his own disciples came to listen to his preaching of the Dharma. It would appear that Shakyamuni did not originally intend to found an extensive religious order and in fact even forbade the monks under him to go about in large groups. He himself took only a minimum number of disciples with him when he went on preaching journeys, his constant concern being the dissemination of Buddhist teachings throughout society as a whole. It is even possible that he trained his disciples primarily so that they might act as teachers to the populace, in which case they best fulfilled his wishes when, after completing their own enlightenment, they ventured abroad to assist in the salvation of the suffering masses.

As a result of these preaching activities, the new religion came to number among its followers not only monks but a large company of lay believers as well. Having taught the Dharma for some forty years following his enlightenment, Shakyamuni had created a wide audience that was eager to listen to his pronouncements. He himself was by this time over seventy, and it would be hardly surprising if at that point he decided to reveal to the world his final understanding of the Truth so that it might be handed down to later ages.

In his closing years, Shakyamuni preached mainly in the vicinity of Magadha, one of the most advanced states in India at the time and a center of intellectual ferment. We may imagine that representatives of the various Buddhist communities scattered about India had gathered in Rajagaha, the capital of Magadha, so as to be near Shakyamuni in his closing years. In the northeast suburbs of the capital stood the hill known as Gridhrakuta or Vulture Peak, and it was there that Shakyamuni preached the Lotus Sutra.

The opening chapter of the Lotus, which serves as the introduction to the work, describes the vast and impressive assembly gathered to listen to Shakyamuni on this occasion. It included, we are told, twelve thousand eminent monks, among them such prominent disciples of Shakyamuni as Anyatta Kaundanna, Mahakashyapa, Uruvela Kashyapa, Gaya Kashyapa, Nadi Kashyapa, Shariputra, and Maudgalyayana; the nuns Mahaprajapati and Yashodhara and their six thousand relatives; eighty thousand bodhisattvas including Manjushri, Avalokiteshvara, Bhaishajya-raja, and Maitreya; the Guardian Kings of the Four Quarters, the Eight Dragon Kings, and Ajatashatru, the king of Magadha.

Picturing this group, we will note that it includes representatives of all the ten realms of existence. The Lotus Sutra is, in a word, an exposition of the basic philosophy of the life force, and it is therefore appropriate that all types of beings should be present at its exposition, as described in the introduction.

With the second chapter, that entitled "Expedient Means," Shakyamuni reveals to the assembly his lifelong desire, namely, that all living beings should attain Buddhahood. Compared to the earlier teachings of Shakyamuni, this represents an epochal departure in the development of the Dharma. Even the disciples who had attended Shakyamuni for over forty years had never until this time dreamed that they could actually become Buddhas. To do so, of course, meant attaining the same lofty realm as their teacher Shakyamuni, which they found difficult to imagine.

Today we are accustomed to thinking of Buddhism as the religion which teaches all beings how to attain Buddhahood. Yet even we, as we take note of our numerous failings and the countless worries that perplex us, can scarcely conceive how we could be qualified to reach such an exalted state. It is not surprising that Shariputra and the other close disciples of Shakyamuni, reflecting in a similar manner upon their own shortcomings, found Shakyamuni much too far above them to think that they could ever equal him. But here was Shakyamuni in his exposition on Vulture Peak declaring that his aim was to bring Buddhahood to all beings. It must have struck his listeners as an earth-shaking pronouncement indeed.

In the "Expedient Means" chapter Shakyamuni declares that "In all the Buddha lands of the ten directions there is only one teaching, not two or three," and he further declares that "All the various Buddhas and World Honored Ones have made their appearance in the world for one single and important purpose alone." They have made their appearance, he goes on to explain, because they wish to awake in all beings the wisdom of a Buddha, to show to all beings the wisdom of a Buddha, to cause all beings to come to a realization of the wisdom of a Buddha, to lead all beings into the wisdom of a Buddha. He even goes so far as to say that "I wish to cause all beings to be the same as myself and to differ in no way." He then proceeds in the chapters that follow to give parables and analogies to illustrate what he means by this, awakening their understanding and predicting that they will attain Buddhahood.

According to the text, Shariputra and the other listeners leaped up and danced with joy when they heard these predictions of the Buddha. And indeed the scene on Vulture Peak must have been one of immense rejoicing, an expression of the life force moving at its most exalted level. Deep within the innermost lives of all the beings who were present, this great gathering and the events that transpired there would be indelibly inscribed forever.

The Shravaka Disciple and the Mahayana Bodhisattva

As we have seen, philological studies indicate that the Mahayana scriptures are somewhat later in date than many of those of the Hinayana school. We come now to the question of why this should be. Do the Mahayana scriptures represent a later stage of growth and expansion within the canon? Or did they exist to some extent from the first, as a line of transmission separate from that which led to the *Agama* sutras of the Theravada school, developing quietly over the centuries and only reaching their present form around the first century B.C.? As I have said, we have no evidence upon which to base a definitive judgment in the matter, and yet it seems to me important at least to speculate.

We have already surmised that Shakyamuni over the course of his fifty years of preaching must have expounded somewhat different doctrines or versions of the Dharma at different periods. If this is so, then we may suppose that his teachings of any given period were handed down after his death in the form of a particular strain or tradition within Buddhist teaching as a whole. This would account for the formation of different types of scriptures reflecting the thought of these different traditions within the religion.

We have also suggested that differences in the content and form of Shakyamuni's teachings would arise depending upon whether they were handed down primarily by the members of the monastic order or by the community of lay believers. The monks, as we have seen, had a tendency to close themselves off from society. With regard to the teachings of Shakyamuni, they appear to have been primarily interested in those dealing with rules of discipline that would serve to maintain order within the monastic community, or with the kind of subtle analysis and interpretation of doctrine that could best be carried out within the quiet and leisure of the monastery. The work of the First Council seems to have been directed mainly at the compilation of such a set of guidelines for the monastic community, and the scriptures of the early schools of Buddhism, which concentrated their interest upon the *Abhidharma*, are similarly limited in scope.

By contrast, we may be sure that when the early followers of the bodhisattva ideal, whose concern was to spread the teachings of Buddhism throughout society, came to compile their scriptures, they placed great emphasis upon those works that would be relevant and appealing to lay believers and members of the populace in general. Many of the Mahayana scriptures are marked by skillful use of parables and other literary forms and are cast in a simple story style that is easy for the general listener to follow, a reflection of the kind of background we have been describing. Since it was the conviction of the Mahayana followers that Shakyamuni had preached not only for the sake of ascetics and members of the intellectual class but for all men and women, it was this latter aspect of his teachings that they strove to maintain and hand down.

Many scholars, rather than viewing these two movements in Buddhism as occurring more or less simultaneously, would regard monasticism as the early form of Buddhism, with the Mahayana movement and its ideal of the bodhisattva arising only later as a reaction against it. Such a view reflects the critical and historical approach favored by most Buddhist scholars today, and if Buddhism is to continue to develop as a world religion, such an objective and historical-minded view of its early development is surely to be encouraged.

However, I feel it is too soon, at least on the basis of the evidence we now have, to declare arbitrarily that the Lotus Sutra and other Mahayana texts are pure fabrications of later ages and have no connection whatsoever with the teachings of Shakyamuni. Mankind's religious insight and inspiration, it seems to me, is too complex and mysterious to be explained away entirely in terms of historical and social background, as modern scholarship too often would attempt to do. It is time that we began to question such tendencies in the scholarship of today. Personally, I find it more reasonable to believe that the basic ideas expressed in the Lotus Sutra and other Mahayana scriptures have their origin in the teachings of Shakyamuni than that they are the invention of later ages, and since there is nothing to disprove my view, I intend to hold to it.

The narrow monastic tendencies deplored by the Mahayana are not something that sprang up only after the death of Shakyamuni, but must already have been present within the Buddhist Order during his lifetime. At that time, we may be sure, there were already those who sought only for their own salvation and neglected the task of spreading the teachings among the lay believers and the populace as a whole. And Shakyamuni no doubt on occasion sharply reprimanded them and attempted to correct their error.

Furthermore, although it is not an argument that pertains to the historical approach mentioned above, we should note that the Lotus Sutra does not simply reject the ideals of the *shōmon* and the *engaku* that had been the goal of the Hinayana monastic communities. The Lotus expounds the principles of the life force, which includes these two among the ten realms of existence. It is a text devoted not to narrow refutations but to the exposition of universal truths applicable to all mankind, which is why it has been so widely read in the past in India, China, and Japan, and continues to be read today.

The Lotus speaks of doing away with the "three vehicles" of the *shōmon, engaku,* and bodhisattva ideals, and replacing them with a "single vehicle" that will offer salvation to all. Some scholars surmise from this that a controversy had broken out in the centuries after the Buddha's death between the proponents of the *shōmon* and *engaku* ideals and those of the bodhisattva ideal, and would regard the Lotus Sutra as an astute invention designed to put an end to controversy by raising the discussion to a higher level embracing both ideals.

This, it seems to me, is an argument that places undue emphasis upon the letter of the text as it took form in writing, without considering how the ideas may have been handed down orally before attaining written form. Moreover, it appears to be based upon the premise that Shakyamuni had no connection with the Lotus Sutra and to be an attempt to bolster that view. As I have indicated previously, however, I cannot accept that premise, no matter how plausible may appear the arguments that are put forward to support it. The reason is that it seems to me to call into question the entire motivation of Shakyamuni in abandoning his family, seeking enlightenment, and preaching the Dharma.

Nearly all Buddhist believers and students of the religion would agree, I believe, that Shakyamuni did not seek enlightenment for himself alone. He sought it in order that he might teach the way of enlightenment to others and free them from the pains and sorrows of human existence. As a result of his religious practices he attained the realization that he himself was a Buddha. And during the following fifty years, when he was preaching the Dharma and attempting to transmit to others the way of enlightenment that belongs to the Buddha, he must, it seems to me, have had as his ultimate goal the awakening in others of the realization that they too are Buddhas. If not, then his mission was meaningless. In other words, to put it in the strongest possible terms, if Shakyamuni died without preaching the universal attainability of Buddhahood expounded in the Lotus Sutra, we can only say that his life was a failure.

The Spread of Buddhism after Shakyamuni's Death

The Ten Major Disciples and the other monks who studied directly under Shakyamuni must have known very well what doctrines he preached at what place and when. And yet, if we accept the viewpoint stated above, we can only conclude that for some reason they failed to understand his most important preachings, those that had to do with the foundation of the life force. In terms of the ten realms of existence that men inhabit, they drew too hard and fast a line of demarcation between the highest realm, that of the Buddha, and those just below it such as the bodhisattva, *engaku* and *shōmon*.

It was the Lotus Sutra that first did away with this line, making clear the fundamental Dharma present in the life force. Thus it became apparent that the Buddha realm is identical with the other nine realms, and vice versa. It also became apparent that all men are equally capable of attaining Buddhahood, and there was no longer any need to question how well the disciples had understood the teachings that Shakyamuni had presented during the previous forty years or to ask whether the lay believers had advanced sufficiently in their religious practices. Even the distinction between monk and layman ceased to be important.

Needless to say, when such a principle of equality is accepted, and both layman and monk are regarded as equally capable of attaining Buddhahood, then the question arises of why one should become a monk at all. In fact we have evidence that doubts concerning this point did arise in the Buddhist Order in the years following Shakyamuni's death and were the subject of prolonged discussion. The *Questions of King Milinda*, for example, contains a discussion of the problem. The venerable monk Nagasena, we may note, concludes the discussion by opining that the lay believer, since he has already carried out various religious practices in his previous existences, is capable of attaining Buddhahood without becoming a monk. This is comforting news to us lay believers, who may presume, I gather, that our austerities have already been completed in previous incarnations.

But to return to a serious note, is there in fact so much difference between the way in which the monk and the layman go about working for the salvation of others? Both are seeking to carry out the Way of the Buddha, and though each, because of his par-

121

ticular manner of life, may pursue the goal in a somewhat different fashion, it is only so that they may cooperate the more effectively. There is certainly no reason for them to act in opposition to one another. And yet, sad to say, the Buddhist community in the years following the death of Shakyamuni seems in fact to have split into two groups, the Hinayana centered around the monastic order, and the Mahayana centered around the lay leaders. And this unfortunate opposition between monk and layman was undoubtedly one of the factors that contributed to the eventual wane and disappearance of Indian Buddhism in the centuries around 1000 A.D.

One may wonder whether Shakyamuni foresaw the danger of such a conflict, and if so, what measures he took to head it off. My own feeling is that, with his remarkable powers of insight, he must have perceived the danger and done all he could to alleviate it. Some indication of this is given in the early scriptures, which describe the rather stern way in which he guided the daily life of the monks who were his immediate disciples, presumably to prevent them from falling into petty factionalism. Undoubtedly the most obvious evidence of his concern is the fact that he gathered together representatives not only from the Buddhist monastic and lay communities but from all walks of Indian life and at Vulture Peak preached the Lotus Sutra with its doctrine of the "single vehicle."

However, in spite of whatever precautions he may have taken, it is an undeniable historical fact that the religious organization which he founded had, some one hundred years after his death, already split into two factions. One cause of this, as I have pointed out a number of times previously, was the fact that the monastic order had allowed itself to become an elitist group isolated from the rest of society. The Mahayana movement, when it came to sudden prominence, claimed that its actions were necessary because the Hinayana schools had turned their backs upon the populace and forsaken the spirit of Shakyamuni's original teachings.

We may suppose, therefore, that the Lotus Sutra and the other Mahayana doctrines taught by Shakyamuni were handed down primarily among the lay believers. They did not come to be labeled Mahayanaist until the great movement by that name brought them into prominence, thereby bringing about a veritable renaissance in the Buddhist religion. But their ideal of the bodhisattva who brings salvation to all beings had all along been a cherished belief among the lay believers of the Buddhist community.

If Shakyamuni correctly foresaw the manner in which his teachings would be transmitted in the years after his death, then he must have realized that it would not be his *shōmon* disciples or their successors in the monastic order who would spread abroad the message of the Lotus Sutra, but the bodhisattvas of the Mahayana tradition. In any event, it is certain that he had constantly in mind the question of who would carry on and spread the teaching of the Dharma after he was gone.

In chapter fifteen of the Lotus Sutra, we find him speaking to the assembly in the following severe manner: "Let it be, good men! You do not need to protect the Lotus Sutra. Why? Because in this world of ours there are great bodhisattvas who are six thousand times the number of the sands of the Ganges, and each of these has relatives who are sixty thousand times the number of the sands of the Ganges. After I am gone, these will guard it for me, will recite it, and will preach this sutra far and wide."

As this famous passage suggests, Shakyamuni was well aware that those who sought to spread his teachings in the years after his death would most likely have to face difficult and trying circumstances. And in fact the preaching of the true Dharma did encounter great hardship in the period following Shakyamuni's death. According to one view, it was political and social opposition to the Buddhist religion that caused the members of the Hinayana to refrain from attempting to spread their teachings throughout society as a whole. In actuality the situation was perhaps such that, even if they had wished to, they could not have effectively challenged the society of the time.

Even during Shakyamuni's lifetime, Buddhism faced a certain amount of opposition and persecution, as indicated by the so-called "Nine Great Ordeals" that Shakyamuni was forced to undergo. Shakyamuni, knowing that the difficulties would be even greater after he had passed away, must often have surveyed his disciples with a feeling of deep apprehension, wondering how many of them would be capable of bearing the hardships in store for them and would have the courage to challenge society. It was perhaps this mood of foreboding that prompted him to remark to them sharply, "Let it be, good men!"

To introduce a new system of thought and make certain that it is transmitted not just fifty or a hundred years, but five hundred or one thousand years, until it has awakened a fire of response in the hearts of men throughout the entire world—this, when we stop to consider it, is a tremendous undertaking. Throughout all of human history in both East and West, there has never been a system of thought that has been transmitted over as great a period of time or space as has Buddhism. And to transmit and spread the teachings of the Lotus Sutra, the highest expression of the Buddhist faith, no doubt required the efforts of a bodhisattva or bodhisattvas of truly extraordinary enlightenment and determination.

9

The Spirit of the Lotus Sutra

Practitioners of the Lotus Sutra

Just how the Lotus Sutra came into being is a question involving a number of historical riddles, at least in our present state of knowledge. This is due in large part to the fact that the Indian people have customarily shown rather little interest in the compiling and preservation of historical records.

But though little may be known about its origin, there can be no doubt of the enormous number of Buddhist believers who have devoted themselves fervently to the task of understanding the Lotus and applying its teachings in their daily lives. The Lotus represents the highest among all of Shakyamuni's expositions of the Dharma, and unless one to some extent is able to enter the realm of the enlightenment of a Buddha, he can hardly hope to grasp its truths. The truths of the Dharma, to be sure, were set forth for the sake of all men. And yet it is no easy matter to discover the correct road leading to them, and one must be prepared to encounter numerous obstacles while pursuing the task.

In the past there have been those who attempted to approach the Lotus from a literary point of view, but they have in the end failed to grasp the ultimate meaning of the Dharma. The realm of religious enlightenment represented by the Lotus can in effect be reached only by pursuit of the correct approach, an intense devotion, and an unflagging attention to practice. To suppose that methods of literary analysis can substitute for these is a fallacy to begin with.

It has traditionally been said that the texts of the Buddhist sutras must be read with the three activities of body, mouth, and mind.

This is true in particular of the Lotus. No matter how many words and phrases of the text one has committed to memory, no matter how eloquently and aptly one may be able to interpret them, if one cannot apply the teachings of the text in one's daily life and translate them into practical and concrete terms of action, then one's understanding of the sutra is valueless.

But what exactly is the practice of the Lotus Sutra? The sutra itself defines it in terms of five actions: preserving the text, reading it, reciting it aloud, expounding it, and copying it. However, it should not be supposed that all five actions are of equal weight and urgency. The first three acts of preservation, reading, and reciting pertain to one's own mastering of the text, while those of expounding and copying have to do with spreading a knowledge of the text to others and insuring its dissemination. But just as the virtue of faith is most consistently emphasized through the Lotus, so the first action, that of receiving and maintaining possession of the text, is the most important of all five.

The men who put together the text of the sutra as we have it today believed without question that it represented the highest expression of the doctrines set forth by Shakyamuni in the course of his lifetime. Chapter two of the sutra tells us that "The World Honored One, after the Dharma has been in existence for some time, will surely expound the Truth." And in chapter ten, the Buddha says, "The sutras which I have expounded number in the countless millions, those I have expounded in the past, those I expound now, and those I shall expound in the future. But among all these, this Lotus Sutra is the most difficult to believe and the most difficult to understand."

These quotations present the idea from the point of view of a number of doctrines of relative merit. In the following quotations, it is presented from the point of view of one absolute doctrine. We have earlier quoted the passage from chapter two that reads, "In all the Buddha lands of the ten directions there is only one teaching, not two or three." And in chapter twenty-one we read, "All the teachings that the Tathagata possesses, all the magical powers that the Tathagata is free to make use of, all the store of secret doctrines of the Tathagata, all the profound affairs of the Tathagata—every one of them is set forth and expounded in this sutra."

The Lotus Sutra is like a great ocean, gathering to itself all the countless rivers and streams, a comprehensive diagram of the life

126

force that underlies all beings. It embraces within itself all other sutras and therefore is supreme. It is designated the highest expression of the Dharma not in comparison to any other expression but because it encompasses the ultimate and most profound principles of philosophy.

The sutra itself overflows with this sense of its own supremeness in its every portion. This, I believe, is because the followers of the Mahayana movement in the centuries after Shakyamuni's death practiced the teachings of the Lotus and had as a result of such practice come to realize its supremacy, had proved the fact of that supremacy to themselves. They had borne the accusations of the followers of the Hinayana, who insisted that "Mahayana is not the Dharma," and had faced other trials and difficulties. And in the course of contending with these tribulations, they had one by one tested the truths of the Lotus Sutra, the profound teachings of the Buddha handed down to them from the past. These followers of the Lotus had in effect experienced with their bodies the text of the sutra.

The Spirit of the Mahayana Buddhists

Some scholars hold the view that the Lotus Sutra represents the doctrines of one group of Buddhists within the Mahayana movement, who, some four or five hundred years after the death of Shakyamuni, fabricated the sutra and attributed it to the Buddha. As I have made clear in a previous chapter, I cannot accept this view, but prefer to believe that the essential ideas of the sutra were handed down from Shakyamuni himself, attracting little attention until they were adopted as the official doctrine of the main body of Mahayana Buddhists.

In the nearly three-thousand-year history of the Buddhist religion, Shakyamuni stands out as a figure of unparalleled greatness. This is because in his enlightenment he was able to grasp in all their fullness the laws of the universe and of the life force within it. During the fifty years of his preaching career he endeavored, by approaching the problem from many different angles, to explain these laws and to bring salvation to all beings. His aim was to lead all beings to the same state of Buddhahood that he himself had reached.

But the principle that all beings are capable of attaining the exact state of Buddhahood attained by Shakyamuni is for the first time clearly enunciated in the Lotus Sutra. Only with the Lotus do we reach what is called in T'ien-t'ai terminology the *enkyō* or "perfect teaching" of the doctrine. Therefore, if Shakyamuni did not in fact preach the Lotus, then we must conclude that he failed to preach the Dharma in its fullest form or to complete the mission for which he came into the world. Such a conclusion is untenable, and therefore I believe that as Buddhists we do best to accept the view that Shakyamuni did preach the Lotus Sutra.

From this it follows that the *Agama* sutras of the Hinayana school and the other Mahayana sutras represent collections of doctrines which Shakyamuni expounded in the years before he at last revealed his true mind in the Lotus. This does not mean, of course, that they are false in any way. They represent revelations of certain aspects of his enlightenment, and as such contain truth, but each is limited to the revelation of only one or another part of the "perfect teaching" embodied in the Lotus.

The question then arises, of course, of why, when the scriptures were being put into order in the years after Shakyamuni's death, it was the *Agama* sutras of the Hinayana school that were first compiled rather than the far more important teachings of the Lotus. I have already touched upon some of the reasons for this, one of the most important being the nature of the organization which took upon itself the task of ordering the scriptures.

In the years immediately after Shakyamuni's death, the first thing that was needed was a set of clear and well-defined rules for the governance of the monastic order, so that organization might carry on the new religion and defend it from the severe attacks and dangers that threatened it. This would explain why the *Agama* sutras, with their attention to precisely such matters of discipline, were the first to be put into order. Later, as the new religious organization secured for itself a stronger and more stable position in society, and as the number of lay believers continued to expand, it could then turn its attention to the compiling of sutras for the householders, that is, to putting into clear and definitive order the Mahayana sutras, with their message of salvation for all beings.

Or we may look at the situation in the following way. The *shōmon* disciples of Shakyamuni, though in the end they were privileged to hear the highest teachings and gain assurance that they would reach Buddhahood, before that received from their teacher instruction in a number of provisional versions of the Dharma. Only after pursuing a long career of study and religious practice were they at last exposed to the "perfect teachings" of the Lotus. They were thus led to the realm of Buddhahood inductively and step by step. On the other hand, the lay believers, who joined the movement at a later date and who, along with their successors, were to become the mainstay of the Mahayana movement in the centuries to follow, were introduced at once to the doctrines of the Lotus, without the preliminary preparation that the monks had undergone. Aided no doubt by favorable karma, they were thus able to attain Buddhahood in one direct and sudden act of recognition.

Does this mean, then, that when the *shōmon* disciples gathered together after Shakyamuni's death to put the scriptures into order, they devoted their attention first to the *Agama* sutras because they were unaware of the importance of the Lotus and the other expositions of Mahayana doctrine?

I think not. If they had been unable to understand the importance of the Mahayana teachings, they could hardly have attained Buddhahood. And one should not forget that the basic ideas later taken over and developed in the Mahayana scriptures are already present in the *Agama* sutras. The *shōmon* disciples, I would surmise, were neither ignorant nor unappreciative of Shakyamuni's Mahayana preachings. But they probably felt that it was not their responsibility to transmit such teachings, or believed that the time to do so had not yet arrived. Therefore the first teachings to become known to the world at large were those of the Hinayana school, while the Mahayana teachings remained in obscurity.

But, as we have seen, by the time some one hundred years had passed after the death of Shakyamuni, the traditional Buddhist organization, with the monastic community as its center, had evolved into a rigid and generally exclusive group. Its members, instead of making an attempt to spread the teachings of Shakyamuni among the populace as a whole, devoted all their efforts to the examination of minute points of doctrine. As a result, those followers of Buddhism, laymen for the most part, who strove to put into practice the bodhisattva ideal found themselves increasingly cut off from the main organization by unbridgeable differences of method and approach.

These doctrinal studies of the monastic community, which took shape in the treatises known as *Abhidharma*, centered around the explication of such concepts as the Four Noble Truths, the Eight-fold Path, or the Twelve-linked Chain of Dependent Origination, and were pursued with the specialists' zeal, while all efforts to bring salvation to the populace in general were neglected. As a result of these tendencies, enlightenment came to be regarded as something that exists only on an extremely lofty plane, and the attainment of Buddhahood accordingly seemed far beyond the grasp of the ordinary monk or layman.

The followers of the Mahayana, on the other hand, viewed the Buddha as a being very close in existence to themselves. Anyone who carried out the practices of the bodhisattva, exerting himself to bring profit and salvation to others, could most certainly become a Buddha. In the Mahayana scriptures, a great number of different Buddhas are described, presumably because the Mahayana followers were capable of perceiving a variety of Buddhas within their own minds and hearts.

There is perhaps another way to look at the division between the Hinayana and the Mahayana in early Buddhism. We may suppose that, during Shakyamuni's lifetime, there were those who were attracted to the new religion mainly because of the outstanding personality of its founder and leader and because of the specifically religious goals and values that it embodied. At the same time, there were those who were principally drawn to it because of its philosophical content. After Shakyamuni's death, the interest in philosophy came to dominate the organization, leading to the *Abhidharma* studies, while the more purely religious activities of preaching and bringing salvation to the population were neglected. And when the early Buddhists lost sight of these religious goals, they in a sense lost contact with the source of the life force that had originally infused the Buddhist religion, the ideal of Buddhahood and the search to attain it.

But one should perhaps not judge the followers of the Hinayana too harshly, for they were bound by their own beliefs. On the whole, for example, they seem to have subscribed to the idea that there is only one Buddha who appears in any given world. After the death of Shakyamuni, the sole Buddha destined to appear in our world, therefore, they had no choice but to spend their lives clinging as tightly as they could to the teachings he had left behind. But, as we have noted, this very devotion to the sutras and rules of discipline in their possession led them into the kind of doctrinal investigation and exegesis that in the end proved arid, while the religious zeal and vitality of the organization gradually drained away.

Meanwhile, the Mahayana followers, comparing the state of the Buddhist organization and its doctrines with the quite different traditions handed down mainly among the lay believers, came to have grave doubts about the validity of the former. For them, the Buddha is a being who is engraved within the heart and mind of all beings and appears in every conceivable world. With this firm faith in the nearness of the Buddha and the attainability of Buddhahood, they set about to spread the teachings of the Mahayana movement and to bring about a renaissance in the Buddhist religion.

The Concept of the Buddha in the Lotus Sutra

The Hinayana concept of only one Buddha for each world is dramatically contradicted in the Lotus Sutra in chapter eleven, where a stupa or treasure tower appears floating in the air over the assembly, and within it are seated side by side Shakyamuni and a second being called the Tahō or Many Treasures Buddha. No doubt the *shōmon* disciples and other followers of Hinayana beliefs in the assembly must have rubbed their eyes in wonder at the sight.

The vision of the stupa miraculously suspended in the air also illustrates another aspect of the Lotus which has troubled some of its more literal-minded readers, namely the element of the fantastic and the irrational. In this connection it may be well to keep in mind the words of Jaspers, who writes, "In order to form a clear image of the Buddha, it is necessary first that the mind be aroused and stirred by a number of striking events the essential reliability of which must be entrusted to the Buddha himself. Only through such a sense of wonder and awe does it become possible for us to visualize him." In other words, the throb of joy aroused in the reader or the hearer brings to sudden life the Buddha that dwells within his own mind and heart.

It is useless to ask whether any such miraculous phenomenon actually took place at the time when Shakyamuni was preaching the Lotus Sutra, nor would there be any point to such a question. The important message to be derived from the passage is that the Buddha world is present within the life force of every single person, and when one's feelings of adoration toward the Buddha are sufficiently strong, these various Buddha worlds within all persons will invariably well up into visible form. For the Mahayana followers living several hundred years after the death of Shakyamuni, at a time when the Dharma seemed to be in danger of disappearing from the world, there was no other course but to try to draw out and visualize the living Buddha that lay within their own hearts and minds. And this intense and devoted search for the Buddha of the mind led them to gather together the Mahayana teachings that had been handed down from generation to generation, to put them into fixed words and phrases, and in this way to compile the text that we know as the Lotus Sutra.

The vision of the treasure tower springing up and hanging in the sky, then, is intended to express this principle of the ability of all beings to realize through their life force the Buddha worlds existing within each of them. At the same time it, and the explanations in the chapters that follow it, serve to refute the old concept of "one Buddha to one world."

Chapters fifteen and sixteen of the sutra in similar fashion present ideas that are highly revolutionary and depart completely from earlier concepts. The first part of the sutra, particularly chapter two on "Expedient Means," is devoted principally to the exposition of the first great universal truth of the work, namely, that all beings of the nine realms other than Buddhahood are endowed with the Buddha nature and contain within themselves Buddha worlds. In chapter sixteen, entitled "The Duration of the Life of the Tathagata," a second great truth is revealed when Shakyamuni explains that he attained Buddhahood many countless eons in the past by practicing the way of the bodhisattva. And the religious practice he followed at that time was none other than the Single Dharma set forth in the Lotus of the Wonderful Law.

This constitutes the most important teaching in the entire sutra. Here we come to understand that it is through faith in and practice of the Lotus of the Wonderful Law that the Buddhas of the three worlds and the ten directions are able to attain Buddhahood. It is the source of all Buddhahood, and without a knowledge of it, Buddhahood can never be obtained.

Before Shakyamuni preached this portion of the sutra, his followers had assumed that he had attained enlightenment for the first time when he left his father's palace, practiced austerities, and at last sat under the Bodhi tree. Now he tells them that "In fact, good men, it is many hundreds of thousands of billions of *nayutas* of *kalpas* since I became a Buddha." One can imagine the astonishment that must have greeted these words.

In spite of such assurance, the *shōmon* disciples apparently continued to think of Shakyamuni's attainment of enlightenment as a unique historical event and to view him as the only Buddha who would appear to preach the Dharma in our present world. Thus, after he died, they felt themselves leaderless and concluded that the most they could hope to achieve was the stage of arhatship through diligent practice of the rules of discipline.

In contrast to this timid and unimaginative view of the Hinayana school, the followers of the Mahayana, particularly those who espoused the teachings of the Lotus, insisted that all beings were capable of attaining Buddhahood and that Shakyamuni had appeared in the world in order to assist them to that goal. Moreover, they averred that Shakyamuni had appeared in many times and places in the past, as when he manifested himself as the Buddha called Burning Light, and though he had, as a means of teaching men, seemed to enter nirvana, he was in fact eternally present in the three worlds of past, present, and future. As he expresses it in the verse portion of chapter sixteen of the Lotus:

In order to save the people
I will show my nirvana to them as an expedient,
But in reality I shall never pass away,
I always live here and expound the Law.

Such is the way in which the Lotus expounds the concept of the Buddha. Through this concept, Buddhism is able to become an eternal light for the guidance of mankind in every age, a faith worthy to spread to every corner of the world. It is this breadth and magnitude of conception that makes the Lotus Sutra unique among the Buddhist scriptures.

The Lotus Sutra's concept of the Eternal Buddha and the numerous manifestations of him that appear in various ages is a highly complex one, and commentators on the sutra have spent much time and effort in expounding its doctrinal subtleties. It is not doctrinal matters that interest me here, however, or a vision of the Buddha as a shining golden figure of eternity. Rather I prefer to envision what Shakyamuni as a man and a religious leader must have been like, a man who no doubt endured far more hardship and suffering than he ever revealed to others, and who was well aware of his own limitations.

Because he himself was a prince of the Shakya clan, many of his disciples were also members of the same aristocratic group in society or young men of the Brahman class. In keeping with its largely upper-class makeup, the new religious organization was able to establish a firm foothold in the society of the time, which was certainly a great advantage to it. At the same time, the fact that so many of the monks of the Buddhist Order were intellectuals of the Brahman class meant that the organization was in many ways cut off and isolated from the needs and interests of the lay believers, who were in many cases of more lowly social status.

Shakyamuni had appeared in the world of ancient India in order to bring salvation to all beings, and yet the religious organization he founded was made up largely of members of the Brahman and Kshatriya or ruler classes. Though they proclaimed the equality of all classes, Shakyamuni's own aristocratic background inevitably colored the thinking of the group and made it difficult to carry out their egalitarian principles in action. This was one of the limitations of early Buddhism as it was established by Shakyamuni, and it continued to be a limitation in the Buddhism carried on by his disciples in the years immediately following his death.

When Shakyamuni, well along in years and nearing the end of his mission, preached the Lotus Sutra, he was probably aware of this limitation. In chapter fifteen of the sutra, the Buddha tells the assembled bodhisattvas that they need not keep and protect the sutra, because innumerable bodhisattvas will spring up from underground to carry out the task of protecting, keeping, reading, reciting, and expounding the text. By this Shakyamuni meant, no doubt, that the Buddhist Order would have to await the appearance of vigorous leaders from the lower levels of society before the doctrine of the equality of all beings and their equal ability to attain Buddhahood could be clearly and firmly established.

Just as the lotus, though it puts forth beautiful blossoms, has its roots in the mud of the pond, so the true practitioner of the Dharma lives and works in the midst of the confusion and bustle of everyday society, sharing the joys and trials of the common people and exemplifying in his way of life the true spirit of the Lotus Sutra. Only in this manner can he carry out the true mission of Buddhism.

10

Nagarjuna and Vasubandhu

Nagarjuna's Search for the Mahayana

In the preceding chapters we have discussed events that took place during the first five hundred years after the death of Shakyamuni. We now move to a somewhat later period to examine the lives of two important thinkers who helped to shape and systematize the doctrines of the Mahayana school of Buddhism. The first was Nagarjuna, a monk of southern India who lived around the middle of the second century A.D., or some seven hundred years after the death of the Buddha. The second was Vasubandhu, known in Chinese also as Tenjin or "Familiar of Heaven," who probably lived in the fifth century A.D. There is much controversy concerning the exact dates of the two men, who are known in Chinese Buddhist texts as Ryūju and Seshin respectively. Here we will attempt merely to discuss the principal legends and philosophical ideas associated with them.

Nagarjuna is famous in later Buddhist literature as the "founder of eight schools." As Buddhism developed in India and in time was transmitted to China and later to Japan, it developed various philosophical schools or sects. Nagarjuna is honored in China and Japan as the founder of eight such schools. Though the exact nature of these various schools need not concern us here, it is an indication of how important was his role in the development of Buddhist philosophical theory.

Nagarjuna's most significant philosophical contribution was the concept of *shunyata*, "emptiness" or "void." This concept has not only had an incalculable effect on the Buddhist thought of China and Japan but in recent years has attracted the attention of Western philosophers as well. Thus, for example, the German Existentialist philosopher Karl Jaspers, in the first volume of the work entitled *Great Philosophers*, lists what he considers to be fifteen of the greatest philosophical leaders of the world; among them are the Buddha and Nagarjuna. For the sake of reference, the remaining thirteen are Confucius, Socrates, Christ, Plato, Augustine, Kant, Anaximander, Heraclitus, Parmenides, Plotinus, Anselm, Spinoza, and Lao Tzu.

Though we may not question the right of the Buddha and Nagarjuna to figure in such a list, we should never lose sight of the fact that they were not merely philosophers in the narrow sense of the word. They were at the same time outstanding religious leaders and practitioners of faith, and it is for this reason that they were welcomed by the populace at large as Buddhas or Enlightened Ones who had come to preach the Truth.

Nagarjuna seems to have lived a very full and eventful life, and we may begin by examining what can be known of it. Our only source is a work in Chinese entitled *Ryūju Bosatsu-den* or *Life of the Bodhisattva Nagarjuna*, which was translated from the Sanskrit by Kumarajiva and is contained in volume fifty of the *Taishō Tripitaka*. According to this work, Nagarjuna was the son of a prominent Brahman family of southern India. He displayed a prodigious talent for learning, at an early age mastering the Vedas and becoming proficient in Brahmanical teachings.

The text then relates the following bizarre incident. Nagarjuna, having completed his studies, was one day discussing with three friends what they might turn their attention to next, and they decided that they should henceforth seek the path of sensual indulgence. Acquiring the art of making themselves invisible, they thereafter began to pay surreptitious visits to the ruler's harem. As a result, one after another of the king's beautiful companions was assaulted, and, to the king's astonishment, some of them in time proved to be pregnant. One evening the king had sand spread outside the gate of the harem and lay in wait for the intruders with a band of soldiers. Though the four young men were invisible, their footprints appeared in the sand when they attempted to enter, and the soldiers sprang after them, slashing the air with their weapons. Pitiful screams were heard, and three of the young men fell dead. Only Nagarjuna managed to avoid injury, by pressing close to the person of the king, and was eventually able to escape from the royal palace unharmed. As a result, he came to realize that passion and

136

desire are the source of suffering, and thereafter made up his mind to become a Buddhist monk.

Whatever we may think of the credibility of such a tale, there is little doubt that Nagarjuna was a man of very strong and unusual personality. This is amply demonstrated by the originality of the so-called *Madhyamika* or Doctrine of the Middle Position, the philosophy which he evolved as a systematization of the concept of the Void found in the Mahayana scriptures. It is this philosophy that has gained him recognition as one of the most important figures in the history of world thought.

Kumarajiva's translation of his biography relates that, after completing his studies in Brahmanism, Nagarjuna became a Buddhist monk and read through the sutras, rules of discipline, and treatises, the three traditional divisions of the Buddhist canon, in a matter of ninety days. But this failed to satisfy him, and he thereupon set off on a journey in search of a deeper understanding of the Dharma. His travels in time took him to the far northern part of India, where he came upon a Buddhist stupa deep in the Himalaya Mountains. There he received copies of some of the Mahayana scriptures from an aged monk and proceeded to read them with great interest, but he continued to feel that there was an even deeper Truth to be discovered somewhere. In order to find it, he traveled about India, engaging in debate with various philosophers and at the same time searching for further Mahayana texts. In view of the difficulties of travel in his time, such extensive journeys must have involved considerable hardship. Yet he pressed on, in the end devoting almost the entire first half of his life to the pursuit of the true Dharma. His determination in the end was rewarded, leading him as it did to the highest peak of Mahayana teaching, that embodied in the Lotus Sutra.

The route by which Nagarjuna reached the Lotus and the other Mahayana teachings may seem a rather devious one, and yet it was probably inevitable. In the world of Indian Buddhism seven hundred years after the death of Shakyamuni, the Hinayana schools, particularly that known as the Theravada or Sarvastivada, still maintained a position of considerable power and importance. Various Mahayana scriptures had already made their appearance to challenge the Hinayana views and practices, but the fact that Nagarjuna had to travel all over India searching for Mahayana scriptures is an indication that the centers of the Mahayana movement were still widely scattered in various regions. Moreover, no truly outstanding Mahayana philosopher or religious leader had as yet appeared to conduct an effective attack upon the Hinayana. This task remained for Nagarjuna himself to accomplish, and with his early training in Brahmanism and Hinayana doctrine and his later espousal of Mahayana, he was ideally suited to carry it out.

Though it falls within the realm of mere speculation, one cannot help wondering how Buddhism would have fared if Nagarjuna had not appeared upon the scene. Surely the voluminous teachings and writings of Buddhism would not have reached China and Japan in nearly as systematized a form as they did. It is true that the Chinese monk Chih-k'ai or Chih-i, the founder of the T'ien-t'ai school, did much to systematize Buddhist doctrine and refine it philosophically, but it is difficult to say how successful his efforts would have been if he had not had Nagarjuna's work to build upon. It is even possible that without Nagarjuna's influence, Mahayana would never have become the dominant school of Indian Buddhism, or that Hinayana doctrine would have persisted for a much longer time in China as a rival of the Mahayana than it did.

In any event, there is no disputing the enormous significance of Nagarjuna's labors, and it is not surprising that as a result of them he later came to be referred to as the "Second Buddha." His particular contribution, it would appear, lay in visiting the many centers of Mahayana activity, which were often isolated from one another, helping them to share and systematize the various scriptures and doctrines in their possession, and to clarify their position in regard to their rivals of the Hinayana. This he accomplished during his travels throughout India, working to shape and lead the Mahayana movement at the same time that he expounded its doctrines and conducted his search for further scriptures. In addition, he debated with exponents of the Hinayana and of non-Buddhist sects and philosophies, exposing the fallacy of their views.

According to the biography of him translated by Kumarajiva, Nagarjuna was eventually led by Mahanaga or the Great Dragon Bodhisattva to the palace of the Dragon King, where he was given "the various Mahayana writings, the most profound scriptures, the wonderful Dharma that is immeasurable." Through his reading of these, he was able to comprehend the deepest truths of the Law. The element *Naga* or "dragon" in his name, represented by the syllable *Ryū* in his Chinese name Ryūju, is said to commemorate this event, and we may suppose that the enlightenment he attained on this occasion was of the very highest order. Incidentally, it may be noted that the second part of his name derives from a type of tree known in India as an *arjuna*. His mother was said to have given birth to him under such a tree, and it therefore became part of his name, the elements *naga* and *arjuna* combining to form Nagarjuna. In Chinese the element *arjuna* is translated simply as *ju* or "tree."

The "most profound scriptures" perused by Nagarjuna would seem to have included nearly all the writings of the Mahayana school. This is evidenced by the quotations from such works that are scattered throughout his voluminous writings. He was in effect a great collector and codifier of Buddhist texts and doctrines, and his writings contain the germs of almost every conceivable theory or philosophical position. As a result, proponents of various later sects have repeatedly proclaimed him the father of their ideas, hoping in this way to lend legitimacy to their teachings. But this represents a misuse of his writings, at least in my opinion. In approaching him, one should attempt to take a broader view, transcending such petty sectarian considerations, and to seek to discover how he has defined the essence of Mahayana Buddhism or delineated the true spirit of the Mahayana bodhisattva. It is with questions such as these in mind that I wish next to examine some of the philosophical concepts of Nagarjuna.

The Theories of the Middle Doctrine and the Void

The biography of Nagarjuna translated by Kumarajiva describes his activities as follows: "He worked to spread a clear understanding of Mahayana abroad, wrote the 'One Hundred Thousand Verses of *Ubadeisha*' [commentary], the 'Five Thousand Verses on the *Sōgon Butsudō-ron*,' the 'Five Thousand Verses on the *Daiji ben-ron*,' and the 'Five Thousand Verses on the *Chū-ron*,' causing the teachings of the Mahayana to flourish greatly in India. He also wrote the 'One Hundred Thousand Verses on the *Mui-ron*.' "

The exact identity and nature of these works need not concern us here. But it is important to note that the *Tripitaka* in Chinese contains a collection of works attributed to "the Bodhisattva Nagarjuna" that totals twenty works in 154 chapters. Nagarjuna was reputed to have lived to be 100, 150, or even 200 years old, but this is still a staggering output for a single individual.

The fact, of course, is that although the collection undoubtedly contains works by Nagarjuna himself, it also includes writings from other hands that for one reason or another have come to be attributed to him. Even in the case of the famous *Mahaprajna-paramitopadesha* or *Daichido-ron*, a one-hundred-chapter commentary on the Mahaprajna-paramita Sutra, which has been quoted earlier, there is some doubt today whether it is actually the work of Nagarjuna. Nevertheless, there can be no question of the great importance and extremely high quality of these philosophical works on Mahayana doctrine which go by Nagarjuna's name.

The Japanese Buddhist scholar Mitsuyoshi Saigusa, in discussing the great importance of Nagarjuna's writings in the realm of philosophy, divides them into five categories. The first consists of the *Chū-ron* or *Madhyamika-karika*, the *Jū'nimon-ron* or *Dvadasha-nikaya-shastra*, and the *Kū-shichijū-ron* or *Shunyata-saptati*. It is the works in this first category that give expression to Nagarjuna's famous concept of the *Chū-ron* or "Middle Doctrine," though references to the concept are also found in works in other categories such as the *Daichido-ron*. Most important is the *Chū-ron* in four chapters, which consists of verses by Nagarjuna and commentary by another monk named Pingala.

The *Chū-ron* begins with a verse of salutation which reads as follows:

The dependent origination
that is not destroyed,
does not come into being,
is not cut off,
is not everlasting,
is not single,
is not plural,
does not come,
does not depart—
this is the highest goodness
that transcends the emptiness of words:
thus did the Buddha teach.
I salute him,
that most eminent
of the expounders of the Way.

Here we are at once presented with the so-called *Happu-chūdō* or

"Middle Path of the Eightfold Negation," which is characterized by the eight negations of non-birth, non-extinction, non-cessation, non-permanence, non-uniformity, non-diversity, non-coming, and non-going.

The first thing to note about this eightfold negation, which sweeps us at once to the heart of Nagarjuna's thought, is that the word "eight" is not intended to be limiting. The meaning is not "eight negations, no more and no less," but rather "numerous negations" or even "infinite negations." It is through this process of negation of every possible concept that one arrives at an understanding of the *shunyata* or "emptiness" that is the core of Nagarjuna's philosophy of the Middle Doctrine.

It is very important to note, however, that the *kū* or "emptiness," which we arrive at through this process of negation, is not the same as mere "nothingness." It is described as "empty" or "void" because we have negated all the possible characteristics or predicates that might ordinarily be used to describe it, but it is totally different in its essential nature from the kind of nothingness that is customarily associated with nihilistic thought. Such a mere nothingness or non-being, which is the opposite of being, would of course in Nagarjuna's thought be negated along with all other concepts. The true "emptiness" of the Middle Doctrine is therefore a nothingness that transcends both non-being and being.

Nothing can be born out of mere nothingness. But from the "emptiness" of the Middle Doctrine, which is a kind of infinite potentiality, anything and everything may be born or produced, depending upon what causes happen to affect it. Various objects and phenomena appear to the ordinary beholder to be arising out of nothing. But what precedes them is not in fact nothingness but the state of *kū* or potentiality that Nagarjuna has been describing.

The philosophical background for this concept of "emptiness" goes back to the so-called Twelvefold Chain of Causation preached by Shakyamuni, which has been described in my earlier volume. According to that, no beings or events exist entirely separately in the world; all are linked to other beings and events through the chain of causation. Nagarjuna demonstrates this aspect of interdependence in his *Chū-ron*, section ten, through the example of fire and firewood. It is a strikingly simple and homely analogy, and at the same time one which helps greatly to clarify the difficult and complex concept of "emptiness" as it functions in his doctrine of the

141

Middle Path. Let us therefore see just how his analogy works.

According to the argument Nagarjuna puts forth, fire cannot burn unless it has firewood to feed upon, and in this sense it must have the firewood in order to exist. Similarly, firewood cannot be called firewood unless fire exists—otherwise it can only be characterized as pieces of wood. In other words, neither fire nor firewood can be said to have any absolute existence independent from one another. And yet at the same time they cannot be said not to exist at all. They exist in the state of "emptiness" or potentiality, waiting for one another to be brought into actual existence.

All beings share this same dependent nature, coming into existence through causation, and it is this that is described by the concept of *kū* or "emptiness." It is neither being nor non-being but a state transcending both.

But although such concepts as causation and emptiness would appear to explain away the nature of all beings and the process by which they come into existence, one should beware of supposing that the situation is really that simple. Nagarjuna, we must be careful to note, says: "We speak of all things as 'empty' which are dependent in origination. But this 'emptiness' is no more than a relative hypothesis. This is the true Middle Path." That is, just as the concept of "emptiness" is arrived at by negating both being and non-being, so the concept of "emptiness" in turn must be negated. The true Middle Path, therefore, consists of this process of perpetual negation. It is an attempt to describe the interdependence of potentiality and place by continually postulating what it is not.

One reason for this emphasis upon negation in Nagarjuna's thought is to be found in the views prevailing in the world of Buddhist thought in his time. The second category of Nagarjuna's writings, as defined by Mitsuyoshi Saigusa in the five-part category mentioned above, includes the works entitled *Vigraha-vyavartani* or *Ejō-ron* and *Yukti-shashthika-karika* or *Rokujūju-nyori-ron*. The purpose of these works is to combat the views of the Theravada or Sarvastivada school of Hinayana Buddhism. This school, still very powerful in Nagarjuna's time, insisted upon the ultimate reality of all phenomena, and devoted its energies to the exposition of the *Abhidharma* in order to support this view. Nagarjuna attempted to expose the error of its assertions by expounding his own view of the "emptiness of all phenomena."

142

In addition, he attacked not only doctrinal errors within Buddhism itself, but also turned his attention to the theories of non-Buddhist schools of philosophy, doing his best to refute those who advocated nihilistic interpretations of the concept of emptiness.

Finally, as we have mentioned already, Nagarjuna emphasized the necessity of moving beyond fixed concepts. In the *Chū-ron* he states: "The various Buddhas sometimes preached the existence of ego, sometimes preached the existence of non-ego, and sometimes preached the existence of neither ego nor non-ego." And in another passage he declares: "Those who cling to the view of 'emptiness only' are incurable!" That is, one must negate not only the concepts of being and non-being, but that of emptiness as well, for only by doing so can one understand the true absence of self-nature that is characteristic of all things, the true nature of "emptiness."

The point Nagarjuna is making here is that one must not allow himself to become the prisoner of mere words such as "dependent causation" and "emptiness" and thereby to interpret the dharmas or phenomena of the world as possessing some fixed and irrevocable nature. To do so is automatically to lose sight of the true "emptiness" or absence of definable characteristics that is their essence. Nagarjuna therefore would insist that one must not understand such concepts as the dependent causation taught by Shakyamuni, or the doctrine of the Middle Path which he himself put forward, in terms of mere words. Rather they are ideals to be realized and made concrete through the unceasing practice of the Way of the Buddha. His philosophy, I believe, should be properly understood not as a system of intellectual terms and concepts but as a program for action.

It is important to note that most of Nagarjuna's numerous writings were in fact the product of actual debates he held with his contemporaries rather than the fruits of solitary speculation. In addition, many of them are devoted to descriptions of the practices appropriate to a bodhisattva of the Mahayana faith. The *Maha-prajna-paramitopadesha* or *Daichido-ron* is more in the nature of an encyclopedia of Buddhist philosophy, but it too in its one hundred long chapters reflects the career of its author, who moved from his youthful study of Brahmanism to an interest in the *Abhidharma* treatises of the Hinayana, and from there, after numerous journeys throughout the country, to a rigorous study of the many Mahayana scriptures that the author had succeeded in searching out and acquiring.

Descartes, after traveling about to many countries, reached his famous conclusion, "Cogito, ergo sum." Nagarjuna, after his extensive search for Mahayana texts, arrived at the belief that "all things are empty." The former is looked up to as the founder of modern Western philosophy, the latter as the father of Buddhist philosophy as it is known in East Asia.

Today Western philosophers are beginning to take a great interest in Buddhist thought, and in the philosophy of Nagarjuna in particular. There are many reasons that might be cited to explain this highly significant phenomenon. Among them is the fact that Nagarjuna, though he lived well over a thousand years before Descartes, had already launched a devastating attack upon the excessive concern with the concept of being, a concept so fundamental in Western philosophy. It is no wonder, therefore, that philosophers in the West, now that they are becoming aware of the nature of his accomplishments, should be anxious to gain a greater understanding of his views.

The Path of Asanga and Vasubandhu

We turn now to a consideration of another major philosopher of Indian Buddhism, Vasubandhu, and his elder brother Asanga.

Like Nagarjuna, Vasubandhu and Asanga were the sons of a prominent Brahman family. They were born in Purushapura in the north Indian state of Gandhara, in present-day Peshawar, probably in the fifth century A.D. Their father, an eminent Brahman teacher of the state of Gandhara, was named Kaushika, and they had a younger brother named Buddhasimha. Vasubandhu and Asanga are known in Chinese translations of Buddhists scriptures by the names Seshin and Mujaku respectively.

All three young men, though trained in Brahmanism, turned their backs on their father's faith and became monks of the Theravada school of Hinayana Buddhism. This is a fact of considerable interest, for it suggests that, although Brahmanism continued to play an important role as the established religion of Indian life, it had ceased to offer the kind of vitality and challenge that would satisfy the spiritual needs of the young. Sensitive and intelligent youths such as Vasubandhu and his brothers, seeking some more progressive doctrine that would allow them full spiritual growth as individuals, turned increasingly to the Buddhist faith.

It must have been something of a shock to Kaushika to see his three sons abandon the religion of their forefathers and become converts to Buddhism, though this sort of action was apparently in accord with the trend of the time. Moreover, a father, if he has the true interests of his children at heart, will always in the long run rejoice to see them embark on more ambitious and venturesome paths than those he himself followed, mindful that in doing so they are being most faithful to the spirit in which he endeavored to bring them up.

The spiritual searchings of Vasubandhu and his brother Asanga did not end with their conversion to Hinayana Buddhism, however, and we soon find them going over to the Mahayana school. Though the two schools existed side by side in the Indian Buddhism of the time, the action of the brothers suggests strongly that the Mahayana was the more dynamic and appealing of the two.

We speak of the Hinayana and Mahayana schools as though these two neat divisions of Buddhism had always existed, and even the terminology we employ expresses a judgement on their relative worth, since the words "Hinayana" and "Mahayana" mean "Lesser Vehicle" and "Great Vehicle" respectively. But in the fifth century A.D. the situation was very different. The superiority of the Mahayana was by no means an accepted fact, and it must have required great courage and conviction for Asanga and Vasubandhu to turn their backs upon the Theravada sect, which proclaimed itself the only orthodox successor to the ancient Buddhist tradition, and join the ranks of the much newer Mahayana movement. They never regretted their choice, however, and for the remainder of their lives they expended every effort in refuting the Hinayana teachings and working to systematize the doctrines of the Mahayana, never slacking in their zeal and devotion.

Asanga or Mujaku in the early years of his conversion to Buddhism is said to have studied the Hinayana view of emptiness as it was expounded by the students of the *Abhidharma*. But he found this unsatisfactory and, employing his supernatural powers, he journeyed to the Tushita Heaven, where he met the Bodhisattva Maitreya and for the first time mastered the Mahayana view of emptiness.

The Bodhisattva Maitreya, who dwells in the Tushita Heaven, the fourth of the six heavens of the world of desire, is often referred to as the Buddha of the future, since it has been predicted that he will appear in the world five billion six hundred and seventy million years after the death of Shakyamuni. At that time he will attain Buddhahood and will become known as the Tathagata Maitreya. According to the traditional account which we have been following, he appeared each evening to Asanga and gave him instruction in the deepest teachings of the Mahayana scriptures.

Granted that there are certain mythical and fantastic elements in the Buddhist scriptures, one is at a loss just how to interpret a passage such as the present one, in which an imaginary being and a historical personage are brought into conjunction with one another. But if we examine the Buddhist canon, we will find a number of texts such as the *Daijō shōgonkyō-ron*, *Chūhen bumbetsu-ron*, *Hōhōshō bumbetsu-ron*, *Gengon shōgon-ron*, and *Yugashiji-ron* that are attributed to Maitreya. One might suppose that they were put together by Asanga, who merely attributed them to his teacher the Bodhisattva Maitreya, and yet there is strong evidence to suggest that they were already in existence before the time of Asanga. My own guess would be that Maitreya was an actual person who acted as the teacher of Asanga. It is quite likely that Asanga referred to him by the name Maitreya out of motives of respect and admiration, implying thereby that he was an incarnation of the Bodhisattva Maitreya. The eminent Buddhologist Hakuju Ui, it may be noted, also looks upon Maitreya as a historical personage, though he adds by way of caution that the whole history of early Indian Buddhism is little more than a tissue of conjecture.

While we may often find ourselves perplexed by the riddles and inconsistencies that seem to beset Buddhist history, as well as the wonders in which it abounds, we must keep in mind that these superficial elements do not affect the validity of the religious and philosophical truths that it embodies. It is here that we most need the quality of faith. The scriptures speak of "using faith to supplement wisdom." It is a basic contention of Buddhist doctrine that the person who has complete faith in the Dharma and practices it without doubt or misgiving will in the end achieve Buddhahood. In other words, the only way to understand the true essence of Buddhism is through the experience and wisdom acquired by actual practice.

Asanga's training in Mahayana doctrine was directed, as we have seen, by Maitreya, perhaps the famous "Buddha of the future," perhaps a monk by that name. There is also a well-known anecdote pertaining to his younger brother Vasubandhu's conversion to Mahayana Buddhism.

Like Asanga, Vasubandhu began his religious career as a follower of the Sarvastivada sect of Hinayana Buddhism. Not as shy and retiring as his older brother, he boldly challenged the proponents of various non-Buddhist philosophies to debate and soon gained considerable fame. Vasubandhu carried out a thorough study of the *Abhidharma* or philosophical treatises of the Sarvastivada sect and compiled a work entitled the *Abhidharma-kosha-shastra* or *Abida-tsuma-kusha-ron*, which presents a systematic and comprehensive discussion of the philosophy contained in them. He thus became the undisputed master of Hinayana philosophy in the India of his time.

We are told, however, that one evening Vasubandhu was listening to one of his elder brother's disciples recite the *Dashabhumika* or Ten Stage Sutra, a chapter of the Avatamsaka Sutra which describes the ten stages of a bodhisattva, when he suddenly gained enlightenment. Filled with remorse for the way in which he had hitherto slandered the Mahayana scriptures, he asked his elder brother to aid him in cutting out his tongue as an act of penance. But Asanga persuaded him to desist from such a rash act, urging him instead to employ the tongue that had earlier defamed the Mahayana scriptures in henceforth praising them. Vasubandhu thereupon vowed that he would never again even in jest recite the *Agamas* or Hinayana sutras and began a new career as a proponent of Mahayana philosophy.

In the Buddhist world of fifth century India, there was continued controversy between the Madhyamika school of Mahayana philosophy, founded earlier by Nagarjuna, and the Hinayana sects such as the Sarvastivada and the Sautrantika, the latter an offshoot of the Sarvastivada. Asanga, following the teachings of his master Maitreya, took over and expanded the Madhyamika philosophy, developing what came to be known as the Yogachara or Way of Yoga school, also called the Vijnanavada or Doctrine of Consciousness. While Asanga was thus engaged, his younger brother Vasubandhu, as we have seen, was expounding the Hinayana doctrines and doing his best to disparage the Mahayana. After his sudden conversion, when he expressed deep regret at his former ways and was forgiven by his elder brother, he joined Asanga as a teacher of Mahayana philosophy.

Taken merely at its surface value, the anecdote reveals the affection that existed between the brothers, particularly Asanga's attitude of forgiveness and solicitude toward his younger brother. But on a more profound level it also conveys the spirit of mercy and tolerance so typical of Mahayana Buddhism. Mahayana's fundamental teaching is a kind of compassion that is capable of embracing and encouraging all forms of life, all types of being. The Hinayana, by contrast, tends to be rather stern and uncompromising in its approach, insisting that evil and delusion be mercilessly cut off. It is one of the most important points of difference between the two interpretations of Buddhism.

One final lesson remains to be extracted from the anecdote, embodied in Vasubandhu's determination to cut out his own tongue because it had earlier denigrated the Mahayana teachings. Though he was fortunately persuaded to desist by his brother, we should keep in mind that a true seeker of the Truth must at all times be possessed of determination and strength of will if he is to fathom the deepest principles of Buddhist doctrine. No halfhearted approach will do.

Thus Vasubandhu joined his elder brother Asanga in becoming a philosopher of the Mahayana school. He is said to have written five hundred works while he was an adherent of the Hinayana, and another five hundred works after he became a convert to the Mahayana. He is therefore known in Buddhist history as the "philosopher of a thousand works."

Asanga was alleged to have died at the age of seventy-five and Vasubandhu at the age of eighty. The Yogachara school of philosophy propounded by the brothers was later introduced to China as the Yuishiki or Consciousness-only sect and continued to flourish in India until the waning and near disappearance of Buddhism from that country. Side by side with the Madhyamika or Middle Doctrine school of Nagarjuna, it constituted one of the two main schools of Buddhist philosophy.

The Kusha and Consciousness-only Treatises

Vasubandhu is reported to have devoted the eighty years of his life to untiring activity on behalf of the Dharma, discoursing with others, writing, and spreading the teachings of Buddhism. He was known, as we have seen, as the "philosopher of a thousand works," though not all one thousand of his writings, if they ever existed, have been handed down to the present. I would like, however, to examine some of the major works that have been preserved and to attempt to assess his importance in the history of Buddhist history and philosophy.

Among his writings on Hinayana philosophy, the most influential text is undoubtedly the *Abhidharma-kosha-shastra* already mentioned above, and the *Jōgō-ron*, a work dealing with the concept of karma. His best known Mahayana works are the *Yuishiki-nijū-ron* and the *Yuishiki-sanjū-ron*, which present a systematic exposition of the views of the Yogachara or Consciousness-only school of philosophy. He also worked to expand and elucidate the ideas presented in earlier works attributed to Maitreya and Asanga, producing many commentaries in this connection. Finally, he wrote commentaries on most of the major Mahayana scriptures such as the *Kongo-kyō* or Diamond Sutra, the *Hoke-kyō* or Lotus Sutra, the *Jūji-kyō* or Ten Stages Sutra, and the *Muryōju-kyō* or *Sukhavati-vyuha*. In these works he deals with such questions as the nature and ten stages of the bodhisattva, the six *paramitas*, and the *tathagata-garbha* or Buddha-nature inherent in all beings.

Of these various works, let us consider first the *Abhidharma-kosha-shastra* or *Kusha-ron*, as it is commonly referred to in Japan. In this work, which Vasubandhu wrote while still an adherent of the Sarvastivada sect of the Hinayana, he presents a critical assessment of the doctrines of that sect as they pertain to the *Abhidharma* treatises, correcting what he looks upon as certain errors in their teachings. Already in this early period of his life it is clear that he disapproved of the tendency in the Hinayana sects to discuss logic and doctrine merely for the sake of discussion, and he accordingly endeavored to return to the spirit of the original teachings of Shakyamuni.

By Vasubandhu's time the Hinayana sects, particularly the Sarvastivada sect, had become firmly established in Indian Buddhism and were well on their way to institutional and doctrinal stagnation. The Sarvastivadins expounded the view that the *dharmas* or elements of phenomenal existence are ultimately real, thus taking up a philosophical position very close to that which Shakyamuni had so strongly criticized in the Brahmans of his time.

Vasubandhu, as we have said, took it upon himself to examine these beliefs of the Sarvastivadins and to pass judgment on them. Thus he analyzed the view advanced by the Sarvastivadins that the dharmas actually exist in the three worlds of past, present, and future, and demonstrated that only the present dharmas, which "keep coming moment by moment," actually exist. From this point of view, he proceeds to present a total of seventy-five dharmas that may be said to exist.

In later times, when Mahayana Buddhism was introduced abroad to China, Korea, and Japan, Vasubandhu's *Kusha-ron* was regarded as essential for an understanding of the basic ideas of Indian Buddhism and was accordingly used as a kind of textbook. Thus Japanese monks would traditionally begin their training with the *Kusha-ron* and other texts of Vasubandhu, and the traditional saying "Peaches, chestnuts three years, persimmons eight years" (that is, peach and chestnut trees take three years to bear, persimmon trees take eight years), in their parlance became "*Yuishiki* three years, *Kusha* eight years." Even men who had devoted their lives to the study and spread of Buddhism needed a period of ten years or more, it would seem, to master the works of Vasubandhu.

All this becomes somewhat ironic when we consider that Buddhism was originally intended to be anything but a program of academic study. Shakyamuni's goal was to bring salvation to every man and woman in society, and though he expounded the principles that he believed should govern human life, he certainly never presented any neat or regularized system of philosophy.

But in order to defend Buddhism from the criticisms of non-Buddhist schools of thought and to provide it with a conceptual framework that would allow it to compete with or take the lead over other religions, it became necessary for Shakyamuni's followers to gather together and put into order the various teachings he had left behind and to shape them into a consistent and comprehensive system of doctrine. In this sense the *Abhidharma* studies, which I have spoken of rather disparagingly up to this point, were a distinct necessity, for they helped to insure the preservation of the Dharma and to defend it from intellectual assault.

Although someone clearly had to undertake this task of pulling together and systematizing the teachings of the Buddha, it was imperative that it be a person who could share the same high level of vision as Shakyamuni himself and who was wholly devoted to the practice as well as to the theory of the Way. Both Nagarjuna and Vasubandhu were such men, as intense in their practice of the doctrine as they were keen in exploring its intellectual ramifications, and thus they were able to complete the undertaking in such a manner as to win acclaim in later ages.

Let us turn now to a consideration of Vasubandhu's Mahayana writings, particularly those giving expression to his *Yuishiki* or Consciousness-only system of thought. In evolving this system of thought, he first set forth the work known as *Yuishiki-nijū-ron*, in which he denied the existence of the external world. All the objects of the phenomenal world, which we ordinarily think of as existing and having specific characteristics, are in fact "empty," purely illusory and lacking any objective existence. In spite of this fact, men in general continue to look upon the objects around them as actually existing. This, explains Vasubandhu, is because the *shiki* or consciousness of the individual beholder creates for him the illusion that they exist. The external world is thus solely a creation of the human consciousness—hence the term "consciousness-only"—and Vasubandhu's explanation of it provides a kind of methodology by which one can come to understand the Mahayana concept of *kū* or "emptiness."

In the earlier discussion of Nagarjuna we have seen how he took a critical approach to the doctrine of the Sarvastivada sect that all entities of the phenomenal world actually exist. Having attained an understanding of the concept of "emptiness" through his own meditation and religious practice, he went on to explain to others that the phenomena of the external world have no objective existence but are in reality "empty," and that the fact of their emptiness must be grasped through the wisdom attained in religious practice. Vasubandhu then pursued the argument by inquiring why men should continue to perceive the external world as real, seeking, as it were, to discover the source from which this persistent delusion derives. He found it in the *shiki* or consciousness of the individual.

Exponents of the Consciousness-only school often use the analogy of a dream or of a spell cast by an enchanter to elucidate their view. Just as the spectators who are under the spell of a magician will mistake a rope for a snake, so the individual, because of the machinations of his consciousness, will mistakenly suppose that the entities of the external world have real existence.

Buddhist philosophy thus becomes increasingly subtle and profound as we move from the teachings of Nagarjuna to those of Vasubandhu. But Vasubandhu himself went a step farther in his work entitled *Yuishiki-sanjū-ron*, in which he sets forth the concept of the *alayavijnana* or *alaya* storehouse of perceptions. In the Hinayana Buddhism of the *Abhidharma* treatises, six distinctive types of consciousness are recognized, corresponding to the senses of sight, hearing, smell, taste, and touch, and the functioning of the conscious mind. In Mahayana Buddhism, however, there are two more types of consciousness, making a total of eight. These two further types of consciousness are the *mana-shiki* or *manas*-consciousness, and the *araya-shiki* or *alaya*-consciousness, both of which are aspects of the subconscious mind. When Mahayana thought was introduced to China, the T'ien-t'ai and Hua-yen schools further elaborated the theory of the eight types of consciousness by adding a ninth type, the *amara-shiki* or *amala*-consciousness, but this point need not concern us here.

The *alaya*-consciousness is a kind of storehouse, which is what the word *alaya* means, in which are contained the seeds that provide the basis for our conceptions of the experiential world. The system of six types of consciousness put forward by the Hinayana, when one examines the foundations of its epistemology, proves to be inescapably idealist in nature. That is, since the conscious mind is the basis of all perception, each individual will perceive the external world in a different way depending upon the workings of his particular mind. With the system of eight types of consciousness, and particularly of the *alaya*-consciousness, however, this difficulty is overcome, and an explanation is provided why all persons in the past, present, and future perceive things largely in the same way. According to this explanation, the seeds of past experience are stored up in the *alaya*-consciousness, and when they are influenced or "perfumed" by outside stimuli, they put forth shoots in the present. Similarly, the experiences of the present are being stored away in the consciousness to become the shoots of the future. Thus all the impressions of the experiential world are the product of seeds stored away in the very foundation of the life force and called into being by external stimuli. And since beings that are generically similar will possess similar storehouses of seeds, they will necessarily tend to perceive the external world in much the same manner.

The Western reader may recall Descartes' famous speculations written in 1619 in "a well-heated room" in Germany in which he speaks of the "seeds" of truth or the "seeds" of knowledge that are present in our spirits as human beings. Modes of thinking and the patterns of life are very different in East and West, and yet it is interesting that two such intellectual giants of Europe and the Orient should both happen to have expressed themselves in such similar fashion. Perhaps it is just another proof that the eternal truths of human life are universal and know no geographical or cultural boundaries.

In the latter half of our present century, scientists all over the world are striving to unravel the secrets of the life force, and this pursuit has led them, particularly those Western scientists who are interested in philosophy and depth psychology, to examine closely the Buddhist doctrine of the Consciousness-only school. Apparently they feel that Vasubandhu's theory of the *alaya*-consciousness may provide an important key in understanding the workings of the life force. It is also reported that doctors who are concerned with the treatment of psychic disorders, those most troublesome of human diseases, have in the process of probing the depths of the patient's psyche been forced to recognize the existence of something very much like the *manas*-consciousness or *alaya*-consciousness described by the Buddhists. It may well be that Vasubandhu and the other philosophers, who lived almost fifteen hundred years ago in India and wrote such voluminous works on their investigations into the mysterious laws governing the life force, may contribute invaluable insights for the understanding of modern man and his civilization.

With this we must conclude our survey of early Buddhism, which began with the events immediately following the death of Shakyamuni and continued down over a period of some one thousand years. We have attempted to cover a vast and complex series of events and developments, many of them very poorly documented, and the treatment has perforce been tentative and sketchy in many places, though I trust that the general outline is sound and without major error or distortion. As research on this and later periods of Buddhist history progresses, I hope at some future time to have an opportunity once again to deal with the topic, for increasingly I feel that men of perception throughout the world today are turning their eyes toward Buddhism and Buddhist philosophy, particularly those branches of it which continue to flourish and retain their vitality in the present age, in search of answers to the fundamental questions of human life.

Bibliography

WORKS IN JAPANESE

On Indian Buddhism
Iwamoto, Yutaka, 仏教入門 [*Bukkyō nyūmon*], Chūō kōronsha, 1973
Masutani, Fumio, 東洋思想の形成 [*Tōyō shisō no keisei*], Fuzambō, 1964
Nakamura, Hajime, インド古代史 [*Indo kodaishi*], 2 vols., Shunjūsha, 1963, 1966
———— インド思想史 [*Indo shisōshi*], Iwanami shoten, 1970
Sasaki, Kyōgo; Takasaki, Jikidō; Inoguchi, Taijun; Tsukamoto, Keishō, 仏教史概説・インド篇 [*Bukkyōshi gaisetsu, Indo hen*], Heirakuji shoten, 1966
Ui, Hakuju, 印度哲学研究 [*Indo tetsugaku kenkyū*], 6 vols., Iwanami shoten, 1965

1. On the Formation of the Buddhist Canon
Kanaoka, Shūyū, 仏典の読み方 [*Butten no yomikata*], Daihōrinkaku, 1970
Maeda, Egaku, 原始仏教聖典の成立史研究 [*Genshi bukkyō seiten no seiritsushi kenkyū*], Sankibō busshorin, 1964
Masutani, Fumio; Umehara, Takeshi, 仏教の思想①知恵と慈悲 [*Bukkyō no shisō: 1. chie to jihi*], Kadokawa shoten, 1968
Shiio, Benkyō, 仏教経典概説 [*Bukkyō kyōten gaisetsu*], Sankō bunka kenkyūjo, 1932
Ui, Hakuju, 仏教経典史 [*Bukkyō kyōtenshi*], Tōsei shuppansha, 1957
Watanabe, Shōkō, お経の話 [*Okyō no hanashi*], Iwanami shoten, 1967

2. On the Theravada and the Mahasanghika
Hayajima, Kyōsei, 初期仏教と社会生活 [*Shoki bukkyō to shakai seikatsu*], Iwanami shoten, 1964

Hirakawa, Akira, 初期大乗仏教の研究 [*Shoki daijō bukkyō no kenkyū*], Shunjūsha, 1969

Katō, Seishin, 大乗仏教の起原及び発達 [*Daijō bukkyō no kigen oyobi hattatsu*], Daizō shuppansha, 1957

Tsukamoto, Keishō, 初期仏教教団史の研究 [*Shoki bukkyō kyōdanshi no kenkyū*], Sankibō busshorin, 1966

3. *On King Ashoka*

Kimura, Kentarō, 小説アショーカ王 [*Shōsetsu Ashōka ō*], Daisan bummeisha, 1973

Kosambi, D. D., インド古代史 [*Indo kodaishi*], Yamazaki, Toshio, tr., Iwanami shoten, 1966

Romila, Thapar, インド史 [*Indoshi*], vol. 1, Kōjima, Noboru; Konishi, Masatoshi; Yamazaki, Motoichi, trs., Misuzu shobō, 1970

Tsukamoto, Keishō, アショーカ王 [*Ashōka ō*], Heirakuji shoten, 1973

4. *On the* Questions of King Milinda

ミリンダ王の問い [*Mirinda ō no toi*], 3 vols., Nakamura, Hajime; Hayajima, Kyōsei, trs., Heibonsha, 1964

Lévi, Silvain, インド文化史 [*Indo bunkashi*], Yamaguchi, Susumu; Sasaki, Kyōgo, trs., Heirakuji shoten, 1958

Nakamura, Hajime, インドとギリシアとの思想交流 [*Indo to Girisha to no shisō kōryū*], Shunjūsha, 1968

5. *On Cultural Exchange between East and West*

Hori, Kenshi, 仏教とキリスト教 [*Bukkyō to kirisutokyō*], Daisan bummeisha, 1973

———— イエスと浄飯王 [*Iesu to Jōbonnō*], Gembunsha, 1968

Masutani, Fumio, 仏教とキリスト教の比較研究 [*Bukkyō to kirisutokyō no hikaku kenkyū*], Chikuma shobō, 1969

Saigusa, Mitsuyoshi, 東洋思想と西洋思想 [*Tōyō shisō to seiyō shisō*], Shunjūsha, 1969

6. *On the Rise of Mahayana Buddhism*

Hirakawa, Akira, *op. cit.*

Miyamoto, Shōson, ed., 大乗仏教の成立史的研究 [*Daijō bukkyō no seiritsu shiteki kenkyū*], Sanseidō, 1954

Nishi, Giyū, ed., 大乗菩薩道の研究 [*Daijō bosatsudō no kenkyū*], Heirakuji shoten, 1968

———— 初期大乗仏教の研究 [*Shoki daijō bukkyō no kenkyū*], Daitō shuppansha, 1945; rev. 1972

Yamada, Ryūjō, 大乗仏教成立論序説 [*Daijō bukkyō seiritsuron josetsu*], Heirakuji shoten, 1959

7. *On Vimalakirti and the Ideal of the Lay Believer*

Hashimoto, Hōkei, 維摩の再発見 [*Yuima no saihakken*], Daizō shuppansha, 1955

────── 維摩経新講 [*Yuimagyō shinkō*], Reimei shobō, 1967

────── 維摩経の思想史的研究 [*Yuimagyō no shisō shiteki kenkyū*], Hōzōkan, 1966

Ishida, Mizumaro, 実践への道─般若・維摩経 [*Jissen e no michi─Hannya, Yuimagyō*], Chikuma shobō, 1965

Kino, Kazuyoshi, 維摩経 [*Yuimagyō*], Daizō shuppansha, 1971

Mushanokōji, Saneatsu, 維摩経 [*Yuimagyō*], Kadokawa shoten, 1956

Watanabe, Shōkō, 維摩経講話 [*Yuimagyō kōwa*], Kawade shobō, 1957

維摩経 [*Yuimagyō*], Ishida, Mizumaro, tr., Heibonsha, 1966

維摩経 [*Yuimagyō*], Nagao, Gajin, tr., Chūō kōronsha, 1974

8. & 9. *On the Formation and Spirit of the Lotus Sutra*

法華経 [*Hokekyō*], 3 vols., Sakamoto, Yukio; Iwamoto, Yutaka, trs. & comm., Iwanami shoten, 1976

Kanakura, Enshō, ed., 法華経の成立と展開 [*Hokekyō no seiritsu to tenkai*], Heirakuji shoten, 1970

Kino, Kazuyoshi, 法華経の探求 [*Hokekyō no tankyū*], Heirakuji shoten, 1962

Ōchō, E'nichi, ed., 法華思想 [*Hokke shisō*], Heirakuji shoten, 1969

────── 法華思想の研究 [*Hokke shisō no kenkyū*], Heirakuji shoten, 1971

Sakamoto, Yukio, ed., 法華経の思想と文化 [*Hokekyō no shisō to bunka*], Heirakuji shoten, 1968

Tamura, Yoshirō, 法華経 [*Hokekyō*], Chūō kōronsha, 1969

Watanabe, Baiyū, 法華経を中心にしての大乗経典の研究 [*Hokekyō wo chūshin ni shite no daijō kyōten no kenkyū*], Aoyama shoin, 1956

10. *On Nagarjuna and Vasubandhu*

現代仏教講座 [*Gendai bukkyō kōza*], vol. 5, Kadokawa shoten, 1955

Hattori, Shōmyō; Kamiyama, Shumpei, 仏教の思想④認識と超越 [*Bukkyō no shisō: 4. ninshiki to chōetsu*], Kadokawa shoten, 1970

Hosokawa, Iwao, 竜樹の仏教 [*Ryūju no bukkyō*], Sankibō busshorin, 1970

Jaspars, Karl, 仏陀と竜樹 [*Butta to Ryūju*], Minejima, Hideo, tr., Risōsha, 1960

Kajiyama, Yūichi; Kamiyama, Shumpei, 仏教の思想③空の論理 [*Bukkyō no shisō: 3. kū no ronri*], Kadokawa shoten, 1969

Saigusa, Mitsuyoshi, 大智度論の物語 [*Daichidoron no monogatari*], Daisan bummeisha, 1973

―――― 竜樹における空の思想・東洋学術研究 [*Ryūju ni okeru kū no shisō, Tōyō gakujutsu kenkyū*], Vol. 11, No. 4, Tōyō tetsugaku kenkyūjo, 1973

Sakurabe, Hajime; Kamiyama, Shumpei, 仏教の思想②存在の分析 [*Bukkyō no shisō: 2. sonzai to bunseki*], Kadokawa shoten, 1969

Ueda, Yoshifumi, 大乗仏教思想の根本構造 [*Daijō bukkyō shisō no kompon kōzō*], Hyakkaen, 1969

Yamaguchi, Susumu, 般若思想史 [*Hannya shisōshi*], Hōzōkan, 1972

―――― 空の世界 [*Kū no sekai*], Risōsha, 1967

WORKS IN ENGLISH

Basham, A. L., *The Wonder That Was India*, New York: Macmillan Co., 1954; Evergreen edition, Grove Press, 1959

Jaspers, Karl, *The Great Philosophers*, 2 vols., Arendt, Hannah, ed.; Manheim, Ralph, tr., New York: Harcourt Brace Javonovich, 1962

The Questions of King Milinda, Rhys Davids, T. W., tr., Sacred Books of the East, Vols. XXXV & XXXVI, Oxford: Clarendon Press, 1890; reprinted by Dover Publications, New York, 1963

Glossary

Where the romanized form of Sanskrit or Pali words appearing in the text differs from the orthodox form, the latter is given in parentheses with full diacritical markings. *S* stands for Sanskrit, *P* for Pali, and *J* for Japanese; words or names not so marked may be assumed to be Sanskrit. Japanese equivalents are given only for the more important names and terms. A few minor place and personal names mentioned in the text have been omitted from the glossary.

Abhidharma, P: *Abhidhamma*, J: *Abidatsuma*. Third section of the Tripitaka (Buddhist canon) containing exegetical and technical works; also called *shastras*

Abhidharma-kosha-shastra (*Abhidharma-kośa-śāstra*), J: *Abidatsuma-kusha-ron*. Treatise by Vasubandhu on the Sarvastivada *Abhidharma* treatises

Abidatsuma (J)   *See Abhidharma*

Abidatsuma-kusha-ron (J)   *See Abhidharma-kosha-shastra*

Agama (*Āgama*) sutras, J: *Agon-kyō*. Four sutras in the Chinese Tripitaka (Buddhist canon); the Theravada (Hinayana) sutras in general

Agon-kyō (J)   *See Agama* sutras

Aiku-ō (J)   *See* Ashoka

Ajase-ō (J)   *See* Ajatashatru

Ajatashatru (Ajātaśatru), J: Ajase-ō.   King of Magadha and son of King Bimbisara

Ajivika (Ājīvika).   Sect deriving from one of the so-called six non-Buddhist teachers

alayavijnana (*ālayavijñāna*), J: *araya-shiki*. The *alaya* storehouse of perceptions

Ambapali, P: Ambapālī.   Courtesan and follower of Shakyamuni

Anan (J)   *See* Ananda

Ananda (Ānanda), J: Anan.   Cousin of Shakyamuni and one of the Ten Major Disciples

Anyakyōjinnyo (J)   *See* Anyatta Kaundanna

Anyatta Kaundanna (P), S: Ājñāta Kauṇḍinya, J: Anyakyōjinnyo.   One of the five ascetics who became Shakyamuni's first disciples

araya-shiki (J)   *See alayavijnana*

arhat, J: *rakan*; *arakan*.   One who has attained the level of saint

arjuna.   A kind of tree (Terminalia Arjuna)

Asanga (Asaṅga), J: Mujaku.   Philosopher and elder brother of Vasubandhu

Ashoka (Aśoka), J: Aiku-ō.   Buddhist ruler of the third century B.C., third monarch of the Maurya dynasty, who unified most of India under his rule

Ashvaghosha (Aśvaghoṣa), J: Memyō.   Indian poet of the first or second century A.D.

Avadana (Avadāna).   Buddhist legends

Avalokiteshvara (Avalokiteśvara), J: Kannon or Kanzeon.   A bodhisattva prominent in Mahayana Buddhism, sometimes called the Goddess of Mercy

Avatamsaka (Avataṃsaka) Sutra, J: *Kegon-kyō*.   The Flower Garland Sutra, an important Mahayana sutra

Avichi (Avīci).   Hell of incessant suffering, lowest of all hells

Benares (Banāras).   City on the Ganges; capital of the ancient kingdom of Kashi

Bhaishajya-raja (Bhaiṣajya-rāja), J: Yakuō.   A bodhisattva in Mahayana Buddhism

Bimbisara (Bimbisāra).   King of Magadha and a follower of Shakyamuni

Bindusara (Bindusāra).   Son of Chandragupta, father of Ashoka, and second ruler of the Maurya dynasty

bodhisattva, J: *bosatsu*.   Highest level of attainment below Buddhahood; the ninth of the ten states of existence

bosatsu (J)   *See* bodhisattva

Brahman (Brāhman).   The priestly class, highest of the four classes of Brahmanic society

Buddha, J: *butsuda*; *hotoke*.   An Enlightened One

Buddhasimha (Buddhasiṃha).   Younger brother of Vasubandhu

butsuda (J)   *See* Buddha

Chakravarti-raja (Cakravarti-rāja), J: Tenrinnō. "Wheel-turning King"; the ideal ruler

Chandragupta (Candragupta). Founder of the Maurya dynasty

Chū-ron (J)　*See Mulamadhyamika-karika*

Daibadatta (J)　*See* Devadatta

Daichido-ron (J)　*See Mahaprajna-paramitopadesha*

Daihatsu-nehan-gyō (J)　*See Mahaparinirvana Sutra*

daijō (J)　*See* Mahayana

Daishu-bu (J)　*See* Mahasanghika

dana (*dānā*), J: *fuse.* Donation, the first of the six *paramitas*

Dashabhumika (*Daśabhūmika*), J: *Jūji-kyō.* Ten Stages Sutra, one chapter of the *Avatamsaka Sutra*

Devadatta, J: Daibadatta. Cousin of Shakyamuni who was a disciple but later turned against him

Dharma, J: *hō.* Buddhist Truth or doctrine

dhuta (*dhūta*), J: *zuda.* Mild ascetic precepts

dhyana (*dhyāna*), J: *zen.* Meditation

Dvadasha-nikaya-shastra (*Dvādaśa-nikāya-śāstra*), J: *Jūnimon-ron.* Treatise by Nagarjuna

Ejō-ron (J)　*See Vigraha-vyavartani*

engaku (J)　*See pratyeka-buddha*

Furuna (J)　*See* Purna

fuse (J)　*See dana*

Gandhara (Gandhāra). Kingdom in northwestern India

gangyō (J). The vow and practice of a bodhisattva

gatha (*gāthā*), J: *ge.* Verse or song, particularly a religious verse or verse portion of a sutra

Gaya-kashō (J)　*See* Gaya Kashyapa

Gaya Kashyapa (Gayā Kāśyapa), J: Gaya-kashō. One of the early disciples of Shakyamuni

ge (J)　*See gatha*

Genjō (J)　*See* Hsüan-tsang

Gion-shōja (J)　*See* Jetavana *vihara*

Gishakussen (J)　*See* Gridhrakuta

goon (J). The "five aggregates" to which all physical, mental, and other elements in the phenomenal world belong: form, perception, mental

161

conceptions, volition, and consciousness of mind

Gridhrakuta (Gṛdhrakūṭa), J: Gishakussen. Vulture Peak, a mountain near Rajagaha in Magadha; sometimes called Eagle Peak

hannya (J)   *See prajna*

Happu-chūdō (J).   Middle Path of the Eightfold Negation, principle of the philosophy of Nagarjuna

haramitsu (J)   *See paramita*

hō (J)   *See* Dharma

Hoke-kyō (J)   *See* Lotus Sutra

hotoke (J)   *See* Buddha

Hsüan-tsang (Hsüan-chuang), J: Genjō.   Chinese monk (600–64) who journeyed to India and wrote an account of his travels

ichinen sanzen (J).   "Three thousand worlds in one instant of life"

Jataka (Jātaka).   "Birth stories," stories of the Buddha in previous incarnations

Jetavana *vihara* (*vihāra*), J: Gion-shōja.   Monastery built by Sudatta at Savatthi

Jōza-bu (J)   *See* Theravada

Jūji-kyō (J)   *See Dashabhumika*

Jū'nimon-ron (J)   *See Dvadasha-nikaya-shastra*

Kalinga (Kaliṅga).   Ancient kingdom in region of modern Orissa

Kannon or Kanzeon (J)   *See* Avalokiteshvara

Kapilavastu.   Capital of Shakya kingdom

Kaushika (Kauśika).   Father of the philosopher Vasubandhu

Kautilya (Kauṭilya).   Minister to the ruler Chandragupta

Kegon-kyō (J)   *See Avatamsaka Sutra*

Kharavela (Khāravela).   King of Kalinga region in first century B.C., a follower of the Jain religion

Koshala (Kośala).   Kingdom in ancient India

Kshatriya (Kṣatriya).   Warrior or ruler class, second highest of the four classes of Brahmanic society

kū (J)   *See shunyata*

Kumarajiva (Kumārajīva), J: Kumarajū, often abbreviated to Rajū.   Famous translator of Buddhist works into Chinese (344–413)

Kumarajū (J)   *See* Kumarajiva

Kū-shichijū-ron (J)   *See Shunyata-saptati*

Kushinagara (Kuśinagara), P: Kusinara, J: Kushinagara. Town where Shakyamuni died

kyō (J) *See* sutra

Kyōryō-bu (J) *See* Sautrantika

Lotus Sutra, S: *Saddharmapuṇḍarīka-sūtra*, J: *Hoke-kyō* or *Myōhō-rengo-kyō*. Most important of all Mahayana sutras

Lumbini (Lumbinī) Gardens. Birthplace of Shakyamuni

Madhyamika (Mādhyamika). "Doctrine of the Middle Position," the philosophy of Nagarjuna

Magadha. Kingdom in ancient India

Mahakashyapa (Mahākāśyapa), J: Maka-kashō. One of the Ten Major Disciples of Shakyamuni

Mahanaga (Mahānāga). The Great Dragon, a bodhisattva

Mahaparinirvana (*Mahāparinirvāṇa*) *Sutra*, P: *Mahāparinibbāna-suttanta*, J: *Daihatsu-nehan-gyō*. Sutra of the Great Nirvana

Mahaprajapati (Mahāprajāpatī), J: Makahajahadai. Maternal aunt of Shakyamuni who became a nun

Mahaprajna-paramita (*Mahāprajñā-pāramitā*) *Sutra*, J: *Maka-hannya-haramitta-gyō*. Large *Prajna-paramita Sutra*

Mahaprajna-paramitopadesha (*Mahāprajñā-pāramitopadeśa*), J: *Daichido-ron*. Commentary on the *Mahaprajna-paramita Sutra*

Mahasanghika (Mahāsaṅghika), J: Daishu-bu. "Members of the Great Order," one of the two major branches of early Buddhism

Mahayana (Mahāyāna), J: *daijō*. "Great Vehicle"; the type of Buddhism practiced mainly in China, Korea, Japan, and Vietnam

Mahinda, S: Mahendra. Prince sent by Ashoka to preach Buddhism to Sri Lanka

Maitreya, J: Miroku. Bodhisattva, often referred to as the Buddha of the future

Makahajahadai (J) *See* Mahaprajapati

Maka-hannya-haramitta-gyō (J) See *Mahaprajna-paramita Sutra*

Maka-kashō (J) *See* Mahakashyapa

mandara-ke (*māndāra-ke*). Mandara flower, red heavenly flower

Manjushri (Mañjuśrī), J: Monju. The Bodhisattva of Supreme Wisdom

Mappō (J). End of the Law, the third and last period following the death of the Buddha

Maudgalyayana (Maudgalyāyana), P: Moggallāna, J: Mokkenren. One of the Ten Major Disciples of Shakyamuni

163

Maurya. Dynasty in early Indian history

Memyō (J) *See* Ashvaghosha

Milindapanha (P: *Milindapañha*). *Questions of King Milinda*, an early Buddhist work in Pali

Miroku (J) *See* Maitreya

Mokkenren (J) *See* Maudgalyayana

Monju (J) *See* Manjushri

Mujaku (J) *See* Asanga

Mulamadhyamika-karika (*Mūlamādhyamika-kārikā*), J: *Chū-ron*. Treatise with verses by Nagarjuna and commentary by Pingala

Muryōju-kyō (J) *See Sukhavati-vyuha*

Myōhō-renge-kyō (J) *See* Lotus Sutra

Nadai-kashō (J) *See* Nadi Kashyapa

Nadi Kashyapa (Nadī Kāśyapa), P: Nadī Kassapa, J: Nadai-kashō. One of the early disciples of Shakyamuni

Nagarjuna (Nāgārjuna), J: Ryūju. Buddhist philosopher of the second or third century A.D.

Nagasena (Nāgasena). Eminent monk who figures prominently in the *Questions of King Milinda*

nehan (J) *See* Nirvana

Nirvana (Nirvāṇa), P: Nibbāna, J: *nehan*. Final state of enlightenment or extinction

Nirvana Sutra *See Mahaparinirvana Sutra*

Nyorai (J) *See* Tathagata

nyoraizō (J) *See tathagata-garbha*

Ōsha-jō (J) *See* Rajagaha

paramita (*pāramitā*), J: *haramitsu*. Reaching enlightenment; practices that lead to the reaching of enlightenment

Pasenadi (P), S: Prasenajit. King of Koshala and a follower of Shakyamuni

Pataliputra (Pāṭaliputra). Capital of the kingdom of Magadha; present day Patna

Pava (Pāva). Village in the Himalayas where Shakyamuni ate the meal that led to his final illness

Pingala (Piṅgala). Fourth century Indian scholar monk

prajna (*prajñā*), J: *hannya*. Perfect wisdom

Prakrit (Prākrit). A simplified form of Sanskrit spoken among the masses

pratyeka-buddha, J: *engaku*. "Private Buddha"; the eighth of the ten states of existence; one who comprehends the Twelve Links of causation but is only interested in his private salvation

Purana Kassapa, (P: Pūraṇa Kāssapa). One of the six non-Buddhist teachers

Purna (Pūrṇa), P: Punna, J: Furuna. One of the Ten Major Disciples of Shakyamuni

Purushapura (Puruṣapura). Birthplace of Vasubandha and Asanga

Rajagaha (P: Rājagaha), S: Rājagṛha, J: Ōsha-jō. Capital of Magadha

Rajū (J)   *See* Kumarajiva

rakan (J)   *See* arhat

ritsu (J)   *See* vinaya

Rokujūju-nyorai-ron (J)   *See* *Yukti-shashthika-karika*

ron (J)   *See* shastra

Ryūju (J)   *See* Nagarjuna

Saddharmapuṇḍarīka-sūtra (S)   *See* Lotus Sutra

Sangha (Saṅgha), J: *sō*. The Buddhist Order or community

Sanzō (J)   *See* Tripitaka

Saptaparna-guha (Saptaparṇa-guhā), J: Shichiyō-kutsu. Cave of the Seven Leaves, in Rajagaha

Sarnath (Sārnāth). Site near Benares where Shakyamuni preached his first sermon to the five ascetics

Sarvastivada (Sarvāstivāda), J: Setsu-issaiu-bu. A school of Hinayana Buddhism

Sautrantika (Sautrāntika), J: Kyōryō-bu. A school of Hinayana Buddhism, offshoot from the Sarvastivada school

Seshin (J)   *See* Vasubandhu

Setsu-issaiu-bu (J)   *See* Sarvastivada

Shakala (Śākala). Capital of the kingdom of King Menander or Milinda

Shakamuni (J)   *See* Shakyamuni

shakubuku (J). To subdue or overcome a mistaken belief, one of the two approaches to be adopted in spreading Buddhist teachings

Shakya (Śākya), J: Shaka. Tribe to which Shakyamuni belonged

Shakyamuni (Śākyamuni), J: Shakamuni. "Sage of the Shakyas"

Sharihotsu (J)   *See* Shariputra

Shariputra (Śāriputra), P: Sāriputta, J: Sharihotsu. One of the Ten Major Disciples of Shakyamuni shastra (śāstra), J: *ron.* Philosophical treatises or commentaries, one of the three divisions of the Tripitaka (Buddhist canon); also called *Abhidharma*

Shichiyō-kutsu (J)   *See* Saptaparna-guha

shiki (J). "Form," one of the *goon*

Shōbō (J). Correct Law, first period following the death of the Buddha

shōju (J). To cultivate or embrace, one of the two approaches to be adopted in spreading Buddhist teachings

shōman (J)   *See shravaka*

Shōman-gyō (J)   *See Shrimala Sutra*

shravaka (*śrāvaka*), J: *shōmon.* One who attains enlightenment by listening to the Buddha's teachings; the seventh of the ten states of existence

Shrimala Sutra (*Śrīmālā-sūtra*), J: *Shōman-gyō.* The Lion's Roar of Queen Śhrīmālā

Shunga (Śuṅga). Dynasty in western India in the second century B.C.

shunyata (*śūnyatā*), J: *kū.* Term often translated into English as "Emptiness" or "Void"; Nichiren Shōshū prefers the more descriptive translation "Potentiality"

Shunyata-saptati (*Śūnyatā-saptati*), J: *Kū-shichijū-ron.* Treatise by Nagarjuna

sō (J)   *See* Sangha

Sudatta. Wealthy man of Savatthi and a disciple of Shakyamuni

Sukhavati-vyuha (*Sukhāvatī-vyūha*), J: *Muryōju-kyō.* A Mahayana sutra dealing with the Pure Land

Sumeru. High mountain that, according to the Buddhist world concept, rises at the center of the universe

sutra (sūtra), J: *kyō.* The scriptures that convey the Buddha's teachings, one of the three parts of the Tripitaka (Buddhist canon)

Tathagata (Tathāgata), J: Nyorai. "Thus Come," a term used for the Buddha

tathagata-garbha (*tathāgata-garbha*), J: *nyoraizō.* The concept of the Buddha-nature inherent in all beings

Tenrinnō (J)   *See* Chakravarti-raja

Theravada (P: Theravāda), S: Sthavira, J: Jōza-bu. "Teaching of the Elders," the type of Buddhism practiced in Sri Lanka and Southeast Asia; also known as Hinayana Buddhism

Tosotsu (J)   *See* Tushita

Tripitaka (Tripiṭaka), J: *sanzō.* "Three Baskets," the Buddhist canon, consisting of three parts: the sutras; the *vinaya*; and the shastras or

Abhidharma

Tushita (Tuṣita), J: Tosotsu. Fourth of the six heavens of the world of desire, abode of the bodhisattva Maitreya

ubasoku (J) *See upasaka*

Upali (Upāli), J: Upari. One of the Ten Major Disciples of Shakyamuni

Upari (J) *See* Upali

upasaka (*upāsaka*), J: *ubasoku*. Male lay Buddhist believer

Urubinra-kashō (J) *See* Uruvela Kashyapa

Uruvela Kashyapa (Kāśyapa), J: Urubinra-kashō. One of the early disciples of Shakyamuni

Vaishali (Vaiśālī). Chief city of the Vajji tribes

Vajji (P), S: Vṛjji. Tribal confederation in ancient India

Vasubandhu, J: Seshin. Buddhist philosopher of the fifth century A.D.

Vedas. Basic scriptures of Brahmanism

Vigraha-vyavartani (*Vigraha-vyāvartanī*), J: *Ejō-ron*. Treatise by Nagarjuna

Vijnanavada (Vijñānavāda), J: Yuishika. Doctrine of Consciousness-only, another name for the Yogachara school

Vimalakirti (Vimalakīrti), J: Yuimakitsu. A rich lay Buddhist believer of the city of Vaishali

Vimalakirti-nirdesha (*Vimalakīrti-nirdeśa*), J: *Yuima-gyō*. Exposition of Vimalakirti or Vimalakirti Sutra

vinaya, J: *ritsu*. Rules of discipline; one of the three parts of the Tripitaka (Buddhist canon)

Yakuō (J) *See* Bhaishajya-raja

Yashodhara (Yaśodharā), J: Yashudara. Wife of Shakyamuni who later became a nun

Yashudara (J) *See* Yashodhara

Yogachara (Yogācāra), J: Yugagyō. The Way of Yoga, a school of Mahayana philosophy

Yugagyō (J) *See* Yogachara

Yuima-gyō (J) *See Vimalakirti-nirdesha*

Yuimakitsu (J) *See* Vimalakirti

Yuishiki (J) *See* Vijnanavada

Yukti-shashthika-karika (*Yukti-ṣaṣṭhika-karika*), J: *Rokujūju-nyorai-ron*. Treatise by Nagarjuna *zen* (J)   *See dhyana*

Zōhō (J).   Imitation Law, second period following the death of the Buddha

zuda (J)   *See dhuta*

zuihō-bini (J).   Principle of adapting Buddhist practices to customs of the local area, provided there is no violation of the main precepts of the doctrine

Index